DR. LEE ANN B. MARINO, PH.D., D.MIN., D.D.

HOW FIRM

CHRONICLES

A
FOUNDATION

Answering What - and Why - We Believe

HOW FIRM A FOUNDATION

ANSWERING WHAT – AND WHY – WE BELIEVE

Dr. Lee Ann B. Marino, Ph.D., D.Min., D.D.

Published by:
RIGHTEOUS PEN PUBLICATIONS
(on behalf of Sanctuary International Fellowship
Tabernacle – SIFT)
www.righteouspenpublications.com

Unless otherwise noted, all Scriptures are taken from the Holy Bible, New International Version, NIV© Copyright © 1973, 1978, 1984 by Biblica, Inc.® Used by permission. All rights reserved worldwide.

Scriptures marked KJV are taken from the Authorized King James Version of the Holy Bible, Public Domain.

Scriptures marked AMPC are taken from the Amplified® Bible Classic Edition (AMPC), Copyright © 1954, 1958, 1962, 1964, 1965, 1987 by The Lockman Foundation. Used by permission. www.Lockman.org

ISBN: 1-940197-65-1
13-Digit: 978-1-940197-65-4

Printed in the United States of America.

This is the House of God

So, we leave politics outside our doors.
We do not argue, nor debate them here
and we respect differences of political opinion.
We do not preach or tolerate hate within these walls,
and we open the door for discussion
of different ideas.
We believe in deliverance and restoration,
and that God's got an answer for anything that ails
you, no matter what it might be –
Spiritual, physical or emotional –
And that we are here for you:
Rich, poor, middle class, or what's next,
Feminist, womanist, black, white, or Hispanic;
Asian, Indian, or indigenous,
Full-figured, plus size, curvy, or thin,
There's no room for shame, we all fit in;
immigrant, refugee, foreigner or wanderer;
LGBT or Q-plus, straight, or in between;
Conservative or liberal,
or whatever falls in the middle;
Married or single, partnered or free;
We all need our found family!
Young or old, or somewhere in between,
Vision is essential for more than we see;
Hoping, expecting, knowing, or still unsure…
We are here to welcome you,
Be your friend, encourage you,
and always remind you:
No matter who you are,
what you've done, what you think,
where you've been,
or what you've walked through –

You are welcome in this place.

TABLE OF CONTENTS

The Serenity Prayer............................... i

Questions and Answers........................ 1

Our Logo.. 92

Statement of Faith................................ 101

Mission Statement................................ 107

Vision Statement.................................. 108

Sanctuary Programs.............................. 109

Info to Help Us Serve You...................... 110

About the Author.................................. 111

God, grant me the serenity
To accept the things I cannot change...
Courage to change the things I can,
And the wisdom to know the difference.

Living one day at a time,
Enjoying one moment at a time,
Accepting hardship as the pathway to peace.
Taking, as He did, this sinful world as it is,
Not as I would have it.
Trusting that He will make all things right
if I surrender to His will.
That I may be reasonably happy in this life,
And supremely happy with Him forever in the
next.
Amen.

(Reinhold Neibuhr, Public Domain)

QUESTIONS AND ANSWERS

Why do we believe in God?

- *In the beginning God created the heavens and the earth.* (Genesis 1:1)

- *God said to Moses, "I AM WHO I AM. This is what you are to say to the Israelites: 'I AM has sent me to you.'"* (Exodus 3:14)

- *To the seven churches in the province of Asia: Grace and peace to you from Him Who is, and Who was, and Who is to come, and from the seven spirits before His throne, and from Jesus Christ, Who is the faithful witness, the firstborn from the dead, and the ruler of the kings of the earth. To Him Who loves us and has freed us from our sins by His blood, and has made us to be a kingdom and priests to serve His God and Father – to Him be glory and power for ever and ever! Amen* (Revelation 1:5-6)

We believe in God because we have known and experienced Him/Her/Them through our faith experience. God has made Himself known to us and we have received that revelation. From the beginning of time to the present and beyond, God, the Creator, has revealed that He is real, active, engaged with us, and cares about His creation.

Why do we believe that God is one?

- *Hear, O Israel: The LORD our God, the LORD is one.* (Deuteronomy 6:4)

- *A Father to the fatherless, a defender of widows, is God in His holy dwelling.* (Psalm 68:5)

- *"The virgin will be with child and will give birth to a Son, and they will call Him Immanuel" - which means, "God with us."* (Matthew 1:23)

- *And I will ask the Father, and He will give you another Counselor to be with you forever - the Spirit of truth. The world cannot accept Him, because it neither sees Him nor knows Him. But you know Him, for He lives with you and will be in you.* (John 14:15-17)

- *…one God and Father of all, Who is over all and through all and in all.* (Ephesians 4:6)

- *For there are three that bear record in heaven, the Father, the Word, and the Holy Ghost: and these three are one. And there are three that bear witness in earth, the Spirit, and the water, and the blood: and these three*

agree in one. (1 John 5:7-8, KJV)

God has consistently revealed Himself to be one throughout salvation history. This is in contrast with other faith systems throughout the world that embrace the idea of many gods (polytheism). We believe in the revelation of God as divine parent (Father, mother), as the Son, Jesus Christ, our redeemer and Savior, and the Holy Spirit (Holy Ghost) as God within us, with us, and through us as our sanctifier and transformer, the way we experience God. Through the roles of Father, Son, and Holy Spirit, we see the entire work of salvation economy: working and bridging the gap as these work as one to fully lead and unite us.

Why do we use masculine, feminine, and gender-neutral pronouns to refer to God?

- *Then God said, "Let Us make man in our image, in our likeness, and let them rule over the fish of the sea and the birds of the air, over the livestock, over all the earth, and over all the creatures that move along the ground."* (Genesis 1:26)

- *And the LORD God said, "The man has now become like one of Us, knowing good and evil. He must not be allowed to reach out his hand and take also from the tree of life and eat, and live forever."* (Genesis 3:22)

- *You deserted the Rock, Who fathered you; you forgot the God Who gave you birth.* (Deuteronomy 32:18)

- *As a mother comforts her child, so will I comfort you; and you will be comforted over Jerusalem.* (Isaiah 66:13)

- *It was I Who taught Ephraim to walk, taking them by the arms; but they did not realize it was I Who healed them. I led them with cords of human kindness, with ties of love; I lifted the yoke from their neck and bent down to feed them.* (Hosea 11:3-4)

- *Jerusalem, Jerusalem, you who kill the prophets and stone those sent to you, how often I have longed to gather your children together, as a hen gathers her chicks under her wings, but you were not willing.* (Matthew 23:37)

- *God is spirit, and His worshipers must worship in spirit and in truth.* (John 4:24)

God does not have gender as we do; such is a human characteristic. God is spirit, and spirit does not have, nor hold gender. Throughout salvation history, God has revealed Himself in different ways that are relatable and understandable to human beings, wherever they might be: as a parent, both as

4

Father and Mother, as "They" and "Us" (because these Three are One), and as *Ruach* (Hebrew, feminine for "spirit") and *Pneuma* (Greek, gender neutral with a strong female association for "spirit"). Through Scripture's revelations to us, we recognize God as everything we identify as, and more, as well as beyond what we can imagine or conceive, because we are made in the image of God.

What is sin?

- *And I will put enmity between you and the woman, and between your offspring and hers; He will crush your head, and you will strike His heel.* (Genesis 3:15)

- *If you do what is right, will you not be accepted? But if you do not do what is right, sin is crouching at your door; it desires to have you, but you must master it.* (Genesis 4:7)

- *What shall we conclude then? Are we any better? Not at all! We have already made the charge that Jews and Gentiles alike are all under sin...for all have sinned and fall short of the glory of God.* (Romans 3:9,23)

- *You see, at just the right time, when we were still powerless, Christ died for the ungodly.*

Very rarely will anyone die for a righteous man, though for a good man someone might possibly dare to die. But God demonstrates his own love for us in this: While we were still sinners, Christ died for us. Since we have now been justified by His blood, how much more shall we be saved from God's wrath through Him! For if, when we were God's enemies, we were reconciled to Him through the death of His Son, how much more, having been reconciled, shall we be saved through his life! Not only is this so, but we also rejoice in God through our Lord Jesus Christ, through whom we have now received reconciliation. Therefore, just as sin entered the world through one man, and death through sin, and in this way death came to all men, because all sinned-- for before the law was given, sin was in the world. But sin is not taken into account when there is no law. Nevertheless, death reigned from the time of Adam to the time of Moses, even over those who did not sin by breaking a command, as did Adam, who was a pattern of the one to come. But the gift is not like the trespass. For if the many died by the trespass of the one man, how much more did God's grace and the gift that came by the grace of the one man, Jesus Christ, overflow to the many! Again, the gift of God is not like the result of the one man's sin: The judgment followed one sin and brought condemnation, but the gift followed many trespasses and brought justification. For if, by the trespass of the one man, death reigned through that one man, how much more will those who receive God's abundant provision of grace and of the gift of righteousness reign in life through the one man, Jesus Christ. Consequently, just as the result of one trespass was condemnation for all men, so also the result of one act of righteousness was justification that brings life for all men. For just as through the disobedience of the one man the many were made sinners, so also through the obedience of the one man the many will be made righteous. The law was added so that the trespass might increase. But where sin increased, grace increased all the more, so that, just as sin reigned in death, so also grace might reign through righteousness to bring eternal life through Jesus Christ our Lord. (Romans 5:6-21)

- *Therefore do not let sin reign in your mortal body so that you obey its evil desires. Do not offer the parts of your body to sin, as instruments of wickedness, but rather offer yourselves to God, as those who have been brought from death to life; and offer the parts of your body to him as instruments of righteousness.* (Romans 6:12-13)

- *If we say we have no sin, we deceive ourselves, and the truth is not in us.* (1 John 1:8)

Sin is a consequence of the fall of mankind, dating back to the experience of Adam and Eve in the Garden of Eden. When given the choice to obey God or defy God and follow the leadings of Satan (the evil one) Adam and Eve chose their own way. Now, as we follow in Adam and Eve's lineage, we all experience sin as part of our lives. None are exempt from it; none are above it. We live in this world and deal with both the results of it as a condition and as perpetrators of it at different times. Sin is this same battle, even today; in the Hebrew, it literally means, "to miss the mark." It lies in the endless numbers of big and little ways we miss God in our lives, thus causing our relationship with Him to be damaged.

We should not despair at the concept of sin. Yes, we do make mistakes and we do live with the results of both our misses and those of others, but God has provided us the answer for sin (even when sin first began to impact humankind). That answer is found in Jesus Christ.

Who is Satan?

- *One day the angels came to present themselves before the LORD, and Satan also came with them. The LORD said to Satan, "Where have you come from?" Satan answered the LORD, "From roaming through the earth and going back and forth in it." (Job 1:6-7)*

- *Then he showed me Joshua the high priest standing before the angel of the LORD, and Satan standing at his right side to accuse him. The LORD said to Satan, "The LORD rebuke you, Satan! The LORD, who has chosen Jerusalem, rebuke you! Is not this man a burning stick snatched from the fire?"* (Zechariah 3:1-2)

- *Jesus said to him, "Away from me, Satan! For it is written: 'Worship the Lord your God, and serve Him only.'"* (Matthew 4:10)

- *The seventy-two returned with joy and said, "Lord, even the demons submit to us in your name." He replied, "I saw Satan fall like lightning from heaven. I have given you authority to trample on snakes and scorpions and to overcome all the power of the enemy; nothing will harm you. However, do not rejoice that the spirits submit to you, but rejoice that your names are written in heaven."* (Luke 10:17-20)

- *Simon, Simon, Satan has asked to sift you as wheat.* (Luke 22:31)

- *I will rescue you from your own people and from the Gentiles. I am sending you to them to open their eyes and turn them from darkness to light, and from the power of Satan to God, so that they may receive forgiveness of sins and a place among those who are sanctified by faith in Me.* (Acts 26:17-18)

- *The God of peace will soon crush Satan under your feet. The grace of our Lord Jesus be with you.* (Romans 16:20)

The term "Satan" means "adversary" in Hebrew. Satan was, once upon a time, an angel in heaven named Lucifer. It was his choice to rebel against God and take one-third of the angels of heaven in rebellion with him. The whole lot were cast out of heaven, to dwell within the realms of hell and wander the earth, tempting and swaying the people of God away from obedience in Him. It was Satan, appearing as a snake or serpent, who tempted Eve to disobey God, with Adam following in suit. Even though some people are afraid of the devil (as Satan is sometimes called) we do not have any reason to fear him, for we have the victory in Jesus Christ.

Why do we believe in Jesus Christ?

- *For to us a child is born, to us a Son is given, and the government will be on His shoulders. And He will be called Wonderful Counselor, Mighty God, Everlasting Father, Prince of Peace.* (Isaiah 9:6)

- *But after he had considered this, an angel of the Lord appeared to him in a dream and said, "Joseph son of David, do not be afraid to take Mary home as your wife, because what is conceived in her is from the Holy Spirit. She will give birth to a Son, and you are to give Him the Name Jesus, because He will save His people from their sins."* (Matthew 1:20-21)

- *In the beginning was the Word, and the Word was with God, and the Word was God. He was with God in the beginning. Through Him all things were made; without Him nothing was made that has been made.* (John 1:1-3)

- *...one Lord ...* (Ephesians 4:5)

- *...that at the Name of Jesus every knee should bow, in heaven and on earth and under the earth...* (Philippians 2:10)

- *He is the image of the invisible God, the firstborn over all creation. For by Him all things were created: things in heaven and on earth, visible and invisible, whether thrones or powers or rulers or authorities; all things were created by him and for Him. He is before all things, and in Him all things hold together. And He is the head of the body, the church; He is the beginning and the firstborn from among the dead, so that in everything He might have the supremacy. For God was pleased to have all His fullness dwell in Him, and through Him to reconcile to Himself all things, whether things on earth or things in heaven, by making peace through His blood, shed on the cross.* (Colossians 1:15-20)

All of us have the option to follow any religious leader found within the world's different religions. One can be selected due to the principles of their teachings, interest in their culture or conduct, or their spiritual ideas. No matter what you might think about religion, Jesus Christ stands out unique among all of them: He is the only religious figure in world history to rise from the dead. Christ, as the Word made flesh, image of the invisible God, and the One in Whom the Godhead dwells bodily is the way by which God has reached out to humanity to "bridge the gap" of sin between us and Himself. Christ accomplished this through His death on the cross and His resurrection from the dead. In Christ, we find that God did for us what we could not do for ourselves. In this understanding, we recognize Jesus is God meeting us where we are.

We also recognize evidence Christ's existence outside the New Testament, by secular sources who acknowledged His existence. No matter what one may personally believe about Christ, no one can question His true influence on history, faith, and the world as a whole.

Why do we believe Jesus is the only way to the Father?

- *The reason My Father loves Me is that I lay down my life - only to take it up again.* (John 10:17)

- *Jesus answered, "I am the way and the truth and the life. No one comes to the Father except through Me.* (John 14:6)

- *Greater love has no one than this, that he lay down his life for his friends.* (John 15:13)

- *Salvation is found in no one else, for there is no other Name under heaven given to men by which we must be saved.* (Acts 4:12)

- *Therefore, since we have a great High Priest Who has gone through the heavens, Jesus the Son of God, let us hold firmly to the faith we profess. For we do not have a high priest Who is unable to sympathize with our weaknesses, but we have one Who has been tempted in every way, just as we are - yet was without sin.* (Hebrews 4:14-15)

- *This is how we know what love is: Jesus Christ laid down His life for us. And we ought to lay down our lives for our brothers.* (1 John 3:16)

- *And they sang a new song: "You are worthy to take the scroll and to open its seals, because You were slain, and with Your blood You purchased men for God from every tribe and language and people and nation. You have made them to be a Kingdom and priests to serve our God, and they will reign on the earth." Then I looked and heard the voice of many angels, numbering thousands upon thousands, and ten thousand times ten thousand. They encircled the throne and the living creatures and the elders. In a loud voice they sang: "Worthy is the Lamb, Who was slain, to receive power and wealth and wisdom and strength and honor and glory and praise!" Then I heard every creature in heaven and on earth and under the earth and on the sea, and all that is in them, singing: "To Him Who sits on the throne and to the Lamb be praise and honor and glory and power, for ever and ever!"* (Revelation 5:9-13)

While many religious leaders might show a way or espouse good ideas, Jesus Christ was the only One Who proved Himself to be love incarnate: willing to lay down His life for those who would follow Him. Through His body, life, death, and resurrection, we can come before God – not on our own merits, but because of what Christ has done for us. We can stand on His merit, His righteousness, and walk in His grace.

What is grace?

- *The Word became flesh and made His dwelling among us. We have seen His glory, the glory of the One and Only, Who came from the Father, full of grace and truth... From the fullness of His grace we have all received one blessing after another. For the law was given through Moses; grace and truth came through Jesus Christ.* (John 1:14,16-17)

- *Therefore no one will be declared righteous in His sight by observing the law; rather, through the law we become conscious of sin.* (Romans 3:20)

- *For sin shall not be your master, because you are not under law, but under grace. What then? Shall we sin because we are not under law but under grace? By no means!* (Romans 6:14-15)

- *So too, at the present time there is a remnant chosen by grace. And if by grace, then it is no longer by works; if it were, grace would no longer be grace.* (Romans 11:5-6)

- *And God is able to make all grace abound to you, so that in all things at all times, having all that you need, you will abound in every good work.* (2 Corinthians 9:8)

- *But because of His great love for us, God, Who is rich in mercy, made us alive with Christ even when we were dead in transgressions-- it is by grace you have been saved…For it is by grace you have been saved, through faith – and this is not from yourselves, it is the gift of God.* (Ephesians 2:4-5,8)

There are many Christians who debate the issue of the law vs. grace, uncertain of the relationship between the two. If we study Scripture, we discover the Old Testament law's purpose was not to be kept, but to make us aware we need a Savior. Through the work of Christ, the law's purpose has been fulfilled. We can receive from God that which we could never do for ourselves: the grace of God. Grace is a complicated concept theologically because it is as much about God and His love and mercy toward us as it is about our own need for God in our lives. Grace recognizes we have missed the mark and gives us the opportunity, yet again, to stand with God even if we don't deserve it. Grace is God's holiness; it is relationship with Him; it is salvation in action; it is spiritual victory this side of heaven. We do not have the grace of God because of anything we've done, because of how good we are, because we go to church, or because we try hard enough. Grace is why we are here, standing with God, empowered to get it right this time, even if we've never gotten it right before. This gift is here because God has given it to us freely through Jesus Christ.

What is repentance?

- *He makes them listen to correction and commands them to repent of their evil.* (Job 36:10)

- *For I take no pleasure in the death of anyone, declares the Sovereign LORD. Repent and live!* (Ezekiel 18:32)

- *From that time on Jesus began to preach, "Repent, for the Kingdom of heaven is near."* (Matthew 4:17)

- *The time has come," he said. "The Kingdom of God is near. Repent and believe the good news!"* (Mark 1:15)

- *I tell you that in the same way there will be more rejoicing in heaven over one sinner who repents than over ninety-nine righteous persons who do not need to repent.* (Luke 15:7)

- *Peter replied, "Repent and be baptized, every one of you, in the Name of Jesus Christ for the forgiveness of your sins. And you will receive the gift of the Holy Spirit."* (Acts 2:38)

- *Repent, then, and turn to God, so that your*

sins may be wiped out, that times of refreshing may come from the Lord, and that He may send the Christ, Who has been appointed for you--even Jesus. He must remain in heaven until the time comes for God to restore everything, as He promised long ago through His holy prophets. (Acts 3:19-21)

The word repent literally means "to turn around, to change direction." Repentance, in a spiritual sense, means our turn or change away from the world of sin and toward the things of God. It also can mean a turning or change of direction, throughout our spiritual walm, from anything that deviates us from God's plan or keeps us from following Him more clearly. In this sense, we "repent," or change direction, constantly throughout our spiritual lives. We repent because there is a promise of restoration to come – the full implementation of the Kingdom of God, throughout the entire cosmos – which we are part of, in part, now, as we await this time to come.

What is new birth?

- *In reply Jesus declared, "I tell you the truth, no one can see the Kingdom of God unless he is born again"... Do not marvel that I said to you, 'You must be born again.'* (John 3:3,7)

- *Praise be to the God and Father of our Lord Jesus Christ! In His great mercy He has given us new birth into a living hope through the resurrection of Jesus Christ from the dead, and into an inheritance that can never perish, spoil or fade - kept in heaven for you, who through faith are shielded by God's power until the coming of the salvation that is ready to be revealed in the last time.* (1 Peter 1:3-5)

- *For you have been born again, not of perishable seed, but of imperishable, through the living and enduring word of God.* (1 Peter 1:23)

- *By which He has granted to us His precious and very great promises, so that through them you may become partakers of the divine nature, having escaped from the corruption that is in the world because of sinful desire.* (2 Peter 1:4)

The new birth is the experience by which a Christian is "born again." We experience this as we come to Christ and submit to His command to repent and be baptized in water, so as to receive the gift of the Holy Spirit. In this experience, we symbolically die to sin and rise again to new life, It gives us empowerment through the Spirit to live for Christ. Our new birth is typified and seen in our baptism in water.

Why do we baptize in water?

- *And so John came, baptizing in the desert region and preaching a baptism of repentance for the forgiveness of sins.* (Mark 1:4)

- *Jesus answered, "I tell you the truth, no one can enter the Kingdom of God unless he is born of water and the Spirit. Flesh gives birth to flesh, but the Spirit gives birth to spirit."* (John 3:5-6)

- *Immediately, something like scales fell from Saul's eyes, and he could see again. He got up and was baptized.* (Acts 9:18)

- *When she and the members of her household were baptized, she invited us to her home. "If you consider me a believer in the Lord," she said, "come and stay at my house." And she persuaded us... At that hour of the night the jailer took them and washed their wounds; then immediately he and all his family were baptized.* (Acts 16:15,33)

- *Crispus, the synagogue ruler, and his entire household believed in the Lord; and many of the Corinthians who heard him believed and were baptized.* (Acts 18:8)

- *Paul said, "John's baptism was a baptism of repentance. He told the people to believe in*

*the one coming after Him, that is, in Jesus."
On hearing this, they were baptized into the
Name of the Lord Jesus.* (Acts 19:4-5)

- *We were therefore buried with Him through
  baptism into death in order that, just as Christ
  was raised from the dead through the glory
  of the Father, we too may live a new life.*
  (Romans 6:4)

- *For we were all baptized by one Spirit into
  one body - whether Jews or Greeks, slave or
  free - and we were all given the one Spirit to
  drink.* (1 Corinthians 12:13)

- *...one Lord, one faith, one baptism.*
  (Ephesians 4:5)

- *In Him you were also circumcised, in the
  putting off of the sinful nature, not with a
  circumcision done by the hands of men but
  with the circumcision done by Christ, having
  been buried with Him in baptism and raised
  with Him through your faith in the power of
  God, Who raised Him from the dead.*
  (Colossians 2:11-12)

- *And this water symbolizes baptism that now
  saves you also - not the removal of dirt from
  the body but the pledge of a good
  conscience toward God. It saves you by the
  resurrection of Jesus Christ, Who has gone
  into heaven and is at God's right hand - with*

angels, authorities and powers in submission
to Him. (1 Peter 3:21-22)

Water baptism is the outward symbol of our inward obedience to Christ. It unites us to Christ in His death as we go down in immersion (fully under water) and are then raised to new life when we are lifted out of the water (symbolic of the resurrection). Through our baptism we receive regeneration: new life, connecting us to the death and resurrection of Christ and His intimate experience therein. For this reason, we believe water baptism is an essential experience for every believer. We believe in its symbolism we experience something sacred.

We perform baptism done in full immersion (enough water for an individual to fully submerse their body under the water, from head to toe). We baptize in the Name of the Father, Son, and Holy Spirit and in the Name of Jesus Christ for the remission of sins, that one would receive the "gift," or "baptism," of the Holy Spirit.

The Scriptures indicate we decide to be baptized because we decide to follow Jesus. To do so, we must have some understanding of why we need Jesus in our lives and the relevance of what He has done for us. There are no instances of proxy or infant baptism within Scripture; to be properly immersed, one needs to have the faculties and physical abilities to handle the rite without drowning. In Biblical times, "household members" would have consisted of recognized adults, such as adult members and household slaves or servants. Nobody should be baptized by proxy, but only when it is a choice they themselves make.

Why do we baptize according to Matthew 28:19 and Acts 2:38?

- *Therefore go and make disciples of all nations, baptizing them in the Name of the Father and of the Son and of the Holy Spirit, and teaching them to obey everything I have commanded you. And surely I am with you always, to the very end of the age.* (Matthew 28:19-20)

- *When the people heard this, they were cut to the heart and said to Peter and the other apostles, "Brothers, what shall we do?" Peter replied, "Repent and be baptized, every one of you, in the Name of Jesus Christ for the forgiveness of your sins. And you will receive the gift of the Holy Spirit. The promise is for you and your children and for all who are far off - for all whom the Lord our God will call."* (Acts 2:37-39)

It is evident from both the New Testament and early church documents that baptism appears to have been performed exclusively in the Name of Jesus. This was in accord with the custom of the times: People were immersed into the system and teaching of their teachers, symbolic of becoming filled with such and raised again within it. While there is some consideration to Matthew 28:19 and Acts 2:38 and conflict, we seek to resolve such, recognizing that within the Name of Jesus is found the fullness of the Godhead; of Father, Son, and Holy Spirit. To reconcile the modern conflicts that exist over interpretation, we baptize according to Matthew 28:18 and Acts 2:38. We also recognize baptisms done exclusively in Acts 2:38.

Why do we have an altar or speak of an altar?

- *Moses took half of the blood and put it in bowls, and the other half he sprinkled on the altar.* (Exodus 24:6)

- *Then burn the entire ram on the altar. It is a burnt offering to the LORD, a pleasing aroma, an offering made to the LORD by fire.* (Exodus 29:18)

- *Then He said, "Here I am, I have come to do Your will." He sets aside the first to establish the second. And by that will, we have been made holy through the sacrifice of the body of Jesus Christ once for all. Day after day every priest stands and performs his religious duties; again and again he offers the same sacrifices, which can never take away sins. But when this priest had offered for all time one sacrifice for sins, He sat down at the right hand of God. Since that time He waits for His enemies to be made His footstool, because by one sacrifice He has made perfect forever those who are being made holy. The Holy Spirit also testifies to us about this. First He says: "This is the covenant I will make with them after that time, says the Lord. I will put My laws in their hearts, and I will write them on their minds." Then He adds: "Their sins and lawless acts I will remember no more." And where these have been forgiven, there is no longer any sacrifice for sin.* (Hebrews 10:9-18)

- *Do not be carried away by all kinds of strange teachings. It is good for our hearts to be strengthened by grace, not by ceremonial foods, which are of no value to those who eat them. We have an altar from which those who minister at the tabernacle have no right to eat. The high priest carries the blood of animals into the Most Holy Place as a sin offering, but the bodies are burned outside the camp. And so Jesus also suffered outside the city gate to make the people holy through His own blood. Let us, then, go to Him outside the camp, bearing the disgrace He bore.* (Hebrews 13:9-13)

The reference to "the altar" is a carry-over from the Old Testament. In the Old Testament, the sacrifices of various animals and offerings proved to be a type, or a shadow, of the work that Jesus Christ would do for us, on the cross. By standing as the sacrificial offering with His own body, Christ has also become our High Priest, mediator with the Father, and ultimate sacrifice, making way for all of us. Today, we recognize the altar as significant of our spiritual need met through Jesus Christ. When we talk about coming to "the altar" or laying something out on "the altar," we are offering ourselves: our lives, needs, and need for Him – significant of our meeting with Him. The altar is where we get real with our Savior and come to Him with a willing heart. It is not the only place we experience His mercy, but a powerful place where the mercy of God meets us if we are willing to humble ourselves before Him. At the altar we find our freedom. It is not always in a church, but wherever God's people gather, and require a spiritual center as they spiritually embrace His work.

Why do we believe in the Holy Spirit?

- *The Spirit of God has made me; the breath of the Almighty gives me life.* (Job 33:4)

- *I baptize you with water for repentance. But after me will come One Who is more powerful than I, Whose sandals I am not fit to carry. He will baptize you with the Holy Spirit and with fire.* (Matthew 3:11)

- *And with that He breathed on them and said, "Receive the Holy Spirit."* (John 20:22)

- *For John baptized with water, but in a few days you will be baptized with the Holy Spirit...But you will receive power when the Holy Spirit comes on you; and you will be My witnesses in Jerusalem, and in all Judea and Samaria, and to the ends of the earth.* (Acts 1:5,8)

- *Peter replied, "Repent and be baptized, every one of you, in the Name of Jesus Christ for the forgiveness of your sins. And you will receive the gift of the Holy Spirit.* (Acts 2:38)

- *Because those who are led by the Spirit of God are sons of God. For you did not receive a spirit that makes you a slave again to fear, but you received the Spirit of sonship. And by Him we cry, <"Abba,> Father." The Spirit Himself testifies with our spirit that we are God's children.* (Romans 8:14-16)

- *There is one body and one Spirit...* (Ephesians 4:4)

The Holy Spirit (God within, among, and around us) is God in our experience. That is because the Holy Spirit is God, working and moving on our behalf in a way we can sense, perceive, and experience in our everyday lives. The Holy Spirit gives us a new sense and awareness of just how real God is; that God is with us, as close as our next breath, surrounding and empowering us to do His work in this world. It is the Holy Spirit that leads us into all truth, comforts us, and ignites us, often depicted as with fire, to purify and ignite us in this time.

Why do believe the Holy Spirit is still alive and active in modern times?

- *For the Holy Spirit will teach you at that time what you should say.* (Luke 12:12)

- *And I will ask the Father, and He will give you another Counselor to be with you forever - the Spirit of truth. The world cannot accept Him, because it neither sees Him nor knows Him. But you know Him, for He lives with you and will be in you.* (John 14:16-17)

- *But the Counselor, the Holy Spirit, Whom the Father will send in My Name, will teach you all things and will remind you of everything I have said to you.* (John 14:26)

- *"'In the last days, God says, I will pour out My Spirit on all people. Your sons and daughters will prophesy, your young men will see visions, your old men will dream dreams. Even on My servants, both men and women, I will pour out My Spirit in those days, and they will prophesy. I will show wonders in the heaven above and signs on the earth below, blood and fire and billows of smoke. The sun will be turned to darkness and the moon to blood before the coming of the great and glorious day of the Lord. And everyone who calls on the Name of the Lord will be saved.'"* (Acts 2:17-21)

- *Exalted to the right hand of God, He has received from the Father the promised Holy Spirit and has poured out what you now see and hear.* (Acts 2:33)

- *Therefore you do not lack any spiritual gift as you eagerly wait for our Lord Jesus Christ to be revealed.* (1 Corinthians 1:7)

- *Love never fails. But where there are prophecies, they will cease; where there are tongues, they will be stilled; where there is knowledge, it will pass away. For we know in part and we prophesy in part, but when perfection comes, the imperfect disappears.* (1 Corinthians 13:8-10)

There is nothing in Scripture that tells us spiritual gifts have ceased. If anything, Scripture tells us spiritual gifts are needed for this time – these "last days," the period between Christ's ascension into heaven (Acts 1) and when Christ shall return. No one knows when Christ is returning, but we do know that while we are here doing the work of the Kingdom, we need spiritual empowerment to complete this task. For this reason, we know the Spirit is alive and active and still at work within God's people, to this day.

What are spiritual gifts?

- *Just as each of us has one body with many members, and these members do not all have the same function, so in Christ we who are many form one body, and each member belongs to all the others. We have different gifts, according to the grace given us. If a man's gift is prophesying, let him use it in proportion to his faith. If it is serving, let him serve; if it is teaching, let him teach; if it is encouraging, let him encourage; if it is contributing to the needs of others, let him give generously; if it is leadership, let him govern diligently; if it is showing mercy, let him do it cheerfully.* (Romans 12:4-8)

- *Now about spiritual gifts, brothers, I do not want you to be ignorant. You know that when you were pagans, somehow or other you were influenced and led astray to mute idols. Therefore I tell you that no one who is speaking by the Spirit of God says, "Jesus be cursed," and no one can say, "Jesus is Lord," except by the Holy Spirit. There are different kinds of gifts, but the same Spirit. There are different kinds of service, but the same Lord. There are different kinds of working, but the same God works all of them in all men. Now to each one the manifestation of the Spirit is given for the common good. To one there is given through the Spirit the message of wisdom, to another the message of knowledge by means of the same Spirit, to another faith by the same Spirit, to another gifts of healing by that one Spirit, to another miraculous powers, to another prophecy, to another distinguishing between spirits, to another speaking in different kinds of tongues, and to still another the interpretation of tongues. All these are the work of one and the same Spirit, and he gives them to each one, just as he determines...then workers of miracles, also those having gifts of healing, those able to help others, those with gifts of administration, and those speaking in different kinds of tongues...But eagerly desire the greater gifts.* (1 Corinthians 12:1-11,28,31)

Spiritual gifts (known in part as the charismatic gifts) are spiritual abilities given through the Spirit for the purpose of edifying and building up the church. Spiritual gifts are freely given by God to whomever God desires, whenever God desires. Spiritual gifts give everyone a job and a place within church, whether a leader or a lay member. This proves God expects us all to work together, giving us all a job to do and a purpose within His church. Our unique combination of spiritual gifts composes our acceptable service to God for His purposes. The Spiritual gifts are: word (message) of wisdom, word (message) of knowledge, faith, healing, miracles (miraculous powers), prophecy, discernment (distinguishing) of spirits, speaking in tongues, interpretation of tongues, administration (government), ministry (service) helps, teaching, exhortation (encouragement), giving, leadership, and mercy.

Why do we speak in tongues?

- *All of them were filled with the Holy Spirit and began to speak in other tongues as the Spirit enabled them.* (Acts 2:4)

- *For they heard them speaking in tongues and praising God.* (Acts 10:46)

- *In the same way, the Spirit helps us in our weakness. We do not know what we ought to pray for, but the Spirit Himself intercedes for us with groans that words cannot express. And He Who searches our hearts knows the mind of the Spirit, because the Spirit intercedes for the saints in accordance with God's will.* (Romans 8:26-27)

- *And in the church God has appointed...those speaking in different kinds of tongues.* (1 Corinthians 12:28)

- *I thank God that I speak in tongues more than all of you.* (1 Corinthians 14:18)

- *Therefore, my brothers, be eager to prophesy, and do not forbid speaking in tongues.* (1 Corinthians 14:39)

Speaking in tongues one gift of the Spirit made available to anyone in the church. To eliminate one gift is to eliminate an important work and purpose of such in the church. We, therefore, uphold tongues as active today, along with other spiritual gifts. Speaking in tongues provides a heavenly language for prayer and sincere people of faith: it unites our words with that of heaven, trusting that what we say is spoken by the Spirit. When one speaks the language of tongues, they are speaking the thoughts and words of heaven. Some believers will speak in tongues privately as part of spiritual prayer; some may also speak in tongues to deliver a spiritual message to the church. When such is done before a church group, someone present must interpret tongues, to help all understand what is said.

Why do we believe in miracles?

- *He performs wonders that cannot be fathomed, miracles that cannot be counted.* (Job 9:10)

- *Remember the wonders He has done, His miracles, and the judgments He pronounced.* (Psalm 105:5)

- *And these signs will accompany those who believe: In My Name they will drive out demons; they will speak in new tongues; they will pick up snakes with their hands; and when they drink deadly poison, it will not hurt them at all; they will place their hands on sick people, and they will get well." Then the disciples went out and preached everywhere, and the Lord worked with them and confirmed His Word by the signs that accompanied it.* (Mark 16:17-20)

- *But if I do it, even though you do not believe me, believe the miracles, that you may know and understand that the Father is in Me, and I in the Father.* (John 10:38)

- *...by the power of signs and miracles, through the power of the Spirit.* (Romans 15:19)

- *And in the church God has appointed... workers of miracles.* (1 Corinthians 12:28)

- *God also testified to it by signs, wonders and various miracles, and gifts of the Holy Spirit distributed according to His will.* (Hebrews 2:4)

Miracles are part of the life of faith. Miracles exist not to change the whole world, but to prove that God is still God. Not everyone receives the miracle they might desire, but all receive the miracle of transformation through faith: salvation by grace through faith, as we experience the love of God.

Why do we believe in healing?

- *Then your light will break forth like the dawn, and your healing will quickly appear; then your righteousness will go before you, and the glory of the LORD will be your rear guard.* (Isaiah 58:8)

- *Heal me, O LORD, and I will be healed; save me and I will be saved, for You are the one I praise.* (Jeremiah 17:14)

- *But for you who revere My Name, the sun of righteousness will rise with healing in its wings. And you will go out and leap like calves released from the stall.* (Malachi 4:2)

- *Jesus went through all the towns and villages,*

teaching in their synagogues, preaching the good news of the Kingdom and healing every disease and sickness. (Matthew 9:35)

- *He called His twelve disciples to Him and gave them authority to drive out evil spirits and to heal every disease and sickness...Heal the sick, raise the dead, cleanse those who have leprosy, drive out demons. Freely you have received, freely give.* (Matthew 10:1,8)

- *...to another gifts of healing by that one Spirit.* (1 Corinthians 12:9)

Much like tongues and miracles, healing is a spiritual gift. Healing is transformed wholeness, often manifest in a way whereas God works in our lives so that we are forever changed. There are many ways that healing manifests in our lives, and it isn't always the way we might like it to happen, nor does it always look like we might expect. Healing is our consistent effort to continue in God's process; to overcome the sin that binds us and affects us as other inflict it upon us; to transform and break through into a state of freedom. Healing many manifest physically, emotionally, mentally, or spiritually.

Why do we lay hands on people in prayer?

- *He could not do any miracles there, except*

lay His hands on a few sick people and heal them. (Mark 6:5)

- *Is any one of you sick? He should call the elders of the church to pray over him and anoint him with oil in the Name of the Lord.* (James 5:14)

Laying on of hands is a powerful point of contact to offer comfort, spiritual power, healing, and miracles to flow. By doing so, one individual believes for God's power on behalf of another. We believe laying on of hands breaks through the isolation and alienation caused by sin; not just alienating us from God, but often, from one another. Laying on of hands is a means of empowerment; of divine appointment and promise, as we receive through and by faith what God has for each of us. In the process the of laying on of hands, we also anoint. Anointing is a symbol of the Holy Spirit, reflecting His fluid power, flowing among God's people. Anointing was also done in Biblical times for medicinal purposes as a balm and comfort to those in need.

When we lay hands on someone, we pray and agree with them for any reasonable and spiritually sound request. We believe God shall do what is best in every situation, and by faith, we stand and believe that whatever God will do is done in Jesus' Name.

What does it mean to be "slain in the Spirit?"

- *Like the appearance of a rainbow in the clouds on a rainy day, so was the radiance around Him. This was the appearance of the likeness of the glory of the LORD. When I saw it, I fell facedown, and I heard the voice of one speaking.* (Ezekiel 1:28)

- *While he was saying this to me, I bowed with my face toward the ground and was speechless.* (Daniel 10:15)

- *And when the disciples heard it, they fell on their face, and were sore afraid.* (Matthew 17:6, KJV)

- *They answered Him, Jesus the Nazarene. Jesus said to them, I am He. Judas, who was betraying Him, was also standing with them. When Jesus said to them, I am He, they went backwards (drew back, lurched backward) and fell to the ground.* (John 18:5-6, AMPC)

- *When I saw Him, I fell at His feet as though dead. Then he placed His right hand on me and said: "Do not be afraid. I am the First and the Last."* (Revelation 1:17)

When someone is "slain in the Spirit" (also called falling under the power, overcome by the spirit, and resting in the spirit) it means they are so overcome by the presence of the Spirit they fall on the ground in a peaceful state, uniquely aware of the presence of God working in and through them. They may fall forward or backward. This is not a scary or chaotic experience, but one by which God moves through an individual. Many who have this experience report visions or prophetic insights while in this spiritual state.

Why do we believe in prophecy?

- *The Spirit of the LORD will come upon you in power, and you will prophesy with them; and you will be changed into a different person.* (1 Samuel 10:6)

- *And afterward, I will pour out My Spirit on all people. Your sons and daughters will prophesy, your old men will dream dreams, your young men will see visions.* (Joel 2:28)

- *The lion has roared - who will not fear? The Sovereign LORD has spoken - who can but prophesy?* (Amos 3:8)

- *For you can all prophesy in turn so that everyone may be instructed and encouraged.* (1 Corinthians 14:31)

- *Then I was told, "You must prophesy again about many peoples, nations, languages and kings."* (Revelation 10:11)

- *At this I fell at his feet to worship him. But he said to me, "Do not do it! I am a fellow servant with you and with your brothers who hold to the testimony of Jesus. Worship God! For the testimony of Jesus is the spirit of prophecy."* (Revelation 19:10)

Prophecy is hearing from God. The words of prophecy reveal the work, will, and thoughts of God to us. Prophecy is an essential aspect of the faith experience: it is the way we learn (by faith) what we shall see to come. It gives us essential insights into where we have been, where we are now, and where we are going. We believe in prophecy because the entire existence of our faith, everything we believe in and trust in by faith, everything revealed to us, and everything yet to come dwells in prophecy.

Why do we believe in apostles, prophets, evangelists, pastors, and teachers?

- *It was He Who gave some to be apostles, some to be prophets, some to be evangelists, and some to be pastors and teachers, to prepare God's people for works of service, so that the body of Christ may be built up until we all reach unity in the faith and in the knowledge of the Son of God and become mature, attaining to the whole measure of the fullness of Christ. Then we will no longer be infants, tossed back and forth by the waves, and blown here and there by every wind of teaching and by the cunning and craftiness of men in their deceitful scheming. Instead, speaking the truth in love, we will in all things grow up into Him Who is the Head, that is, Christ. From Him the whole body, joined and held together by every supporting ligament, grows and builds itself up in love, as each part does its work.* (Ephesians 4:11-16)

- *And in the church God has appointed first of all apostles, second prophets, third teachers...* (1 Corinthians 12:28)

- *Consequently, you are no longer foreigners and aliens, but fellow citizens with God's people and members of God's household, built on the foundation of the apostles and prophets, with Christ Jesus Himself as the chief cornerstone.* (Ephesians 2:19-20)

- *Rejoice over her, O heaven! Rejoice, saints and apostles and prophets! God has judged her for the way she treated you.'"* (Revelation 18:20)

The Scriptures reveal to us the New Testament model of church leadership, found in Ephesians 4:11: Apostle, prophet, evangelist, pastor, and teacher. This is sometimes called the "Ephesians

4:11 leadership model" or "the five-fold ministry." The offices of Ephesians 4:11 are spoken of as gifts, sometimes as the "ascension gifts" because they were given to the church in the ascension of Christ. By doing so, Christ left His ministry to the church, now within the body of believers, rather than remaining exclusively within His being. These gifts are teaching gifts and are not open to everyone in the church. God calls leaders to serve in these roles, established before the foundations of the world. In the New Testament, we see the work of apostles (those who are sent with a special message to lead the church), prophets (those who speak for God), evangelists (those who preach Christ), pastors (those who shepherd or lead lay members of a church), and teachers (those who teach) at work, building the church in its infancy. Today, we refer to this model of leadership as "apostolic," because it first started with the apostles of Christ (the foundation of the church is the apostles and prophets). We continue in this model of church leadership throughout the world, as we continue to establish and build what God has in store for us from now until the time when Jesus returns.

Why do we believe in the work of bishops (overseers), elders, and deacons?

- *"Brothers, choose seven men from among you who are known to be full of the Spirit and wisdom. We will turn this responsibility over to them and will give our attention to prayer and the ministry of the word." This proposal pleased the whole group. They chose Stephen, a man full of faith and of the Holy Spirit; also Philip, Procorus, Nicanor, Timon, Parmenas, and Nicolas from Antioch, a convert to Judaism. They presented these men to the apostles, who prayed and laid their hands on them.* (Acts 6:3-6)

- *Paul and Timothy, servants of Christ Jesus, To all the saints in Christ Jesus at Philippi, together with the overseers and deacons...* (Philippians 1:1)

- *Here is a trustworthy saying: If anyone sets his heart on being an overseer, he desires a noble task... Deacons, likewise, are to be men worthy of respect, sincere, not indulging in much wine, and not pursuing dishonest gain.* (1 Timothy 3:1,8)

- *The elders who direct the affairs of the church well are worthy of double honor, especially those whose work is preaching and teaching.* (1 Timothy 5:17)

- *The reason I left you in Crete was that you might straighten out what was left unfinished and appoint elders in every town, as I directed you.* (Titus 1:5)

- *Since an overseer is entrusted with God's work, he must be blameless - not overbearing, not quick-tempered, not given to drunkenness, not violent, not pursuing dishonest gain.* (Titus 1:7)

- *You must teach what is in accord with sound doctrine. Teach the older men to be temperate, worthy of respect, self-controlled, and sound in faith, in love and in endurance. Likewise, teach the older women to be reverent in the way they live, not to be slanderers or addicted to much wine, but to teach what is good. Then they can train the younger women to love their husbands and children, to be self-controlled and pure, to be busy at home, to be kind, and to be subject to their husbands, so that no one will malign the word of God. Similarly, encourage the young men to be self-controlled.* (Titus 2:2-6)

- *To the elders among you, I appeal as a fellow elder, a witness of Christ's sufferings and one who also will share in the glory to be revealed.* (1 Peter 5:1)

- *Surrounding the throne were twenty-four other thrones, and seated on them were twenty-four elders. They were dressed in white and had crowns of gold on their heads.* (Revelation 4:4)

Bishops, elders, and deacons form the work of the

appointment ministries, sometimes called the appointments. They are called "appointments" because such positions are not a calling. They are, instead, an appointment; something one is appointed to do. These three ministry works are leaders over the helps, or assistance for the necessary works (needs) of the church. Bishops assist apostles, elders assist pastors, and deacons serve the entire body of believers, both leadership and laity. Scripture outlines more criteria for serving in the appointment ministries than in the Ephesians 4:11 model, simply to teach us that it is important to establish criteria for those who desire to help. The appointment ministries are appointed by apostles.

Why do we believe in the gifting attributes of the Spirit?

- *The Spirit of the LORD will rest on Him - the Spirit of wisdom and of understanding, the Spirit of counsel and of power, the Spirit of knowledge and of the fear of the LORD - and He will delight in the fear of the LORD. He will not judge by what He sees with His eyes, or decide by what He hears with his ears; but with righteousness He will judge the needy, with justice He will give decisions for the poor of the earth. He will strike the earth with the rod of His mouth; with the breath of His lips He will slay the wicked. Righteousness will be*

His belt and faithfulness the sash around His waist. (Isaiah 11:2-5)

The gifting attributes of the Spirit are specific things the Holy Spirit does within us that relate to our character. When we are in Christ, we also reflect and adopt His nature as our own. These specific attributes reflect the true character of God. These are wisdom, understanding, counsel, strength (power), knowledge and fear of the Lord. The results of these attributes are delighting in the fear of the Lord, right judgment, righteousness, justice, and faithfulness.

Why do we believe in prophetic expressions?

- *Every skilled woman spun with her hands and brought what she had spun - blue, purple or scarlet yarn or fine linen. And all the women who were willing and had the skill spun the goat hair... Then Moses said to the Israelites, "See, the LORD has chosen Bezalel son of Uri, the son of Hur, of the tribe of Judah, and he has filled him with the Spirit of God, with skill, ability and knowledge in all kinds of crafts - to make artistic designs for work in gold, silver and bronze, to cut and set stones, to work in wood and to engage in all kinds of artistic craftsmanship.* (Exodus 35:23-26,30-33)

- *David, wearing a linen ephod, danced before the LORD with all his might.* (2 Samuel 6:14)

- *Rizpah daughter of Aiah took sackcloth and spread it out for herself on a rock. From the beginning of the harvest till the rain poured down from the heavens on the bodies, she did not let the birds of the air touch them by day or the wild animals by night.* (2 Samuel 21:10)

- *All the Levites who were musicians - Asaph, Heman, Jeduthun and their sons and relatives - stood on the east side of the altar, dressed in fine linen and playing cymbals, harps and lyres. They were accompanied by 120 priests sounding trumpets. The trumpeters and singers joined in unison, as with one voice, to give praise and thanks to the LORD. Accompanied by trumpets, cymbals and other instruments, they raised their voices in praise to the LORD and sang: "He is good; His love endures forever." Then the temple of the LORD was filled with a cloud, and the priests could not perform their service because of the cloud, for the glory of the LORD filled the temple of God.* (2 Chronicles 5:12-14)

- *For the director of music. To [the tune of] "Lilies." Of the Sons of Korah. A wedding song. My heart is stirred by a noble theme as I recite my verses for the king; my tongue is the pen of a skillful writer.* (Psalm 45:1)

- *Let them praise His Name with dancing and make music to Him with tambourine and harp.* (Psalm 149:3)

- *During the daytime, while they watch, bring out your belongings packed for exile. Then in the evening, while they are watching, go out like those who go into exile. While they watch, dig through the wall and take your belongings out through it. Put them on your shoulder as they are watching and carry them out at dusk. Cover your face so that you cannot see the land, for I have made you a sign to the house of Israel.* (Ezekiel 12:3-6)

- *I am not writing this to shame you, but to warn you, as my dear children.* (1 Corinthians 4:14)

- *Therefore He is able to save completely those who come to God through Him, because He always lives to intercede for them.* (Hebrews 7:25)

Prophetic expressions are different ways the Spirit expresses Himself/Herself/Themself, making Himself/Herself/Themself manifest to God's people in many creative ways. These are not performances, but abilities provided by the Spirit to help draw us into the place of God and make the presence of God known. We believe in them because we see them clearly manifest as God moves through His people.

These are intercession, testimony, skilled design, visual arts, music, drama, dance, writing, and inspiration.

What do we believe are the functions of the church?

- *"We both had dreams," they answered, "but there is no one to interpret them." Then Joseph said to them, "Do not interpretations belong to God? Tell me your dreams."* (Genesis 40:8)

- *Then Samuel said, "Assemble all Israel at Mizpah and I will intercede with the LORD for you."* (1 Samuel 7:5)

- *The watchman called out to the king and reported it.* (2 Samuel 18:25)

- *Then the king of Assyria gave this order: "Have one of the priests you took captive from Samaria go back to live there and teach the people what the god of the land requires." So one of the priests who had been exiled from Samaria came to live in Bethel and taught them how to worship the LORD.* (2 Kings 17:27-28)

- *The gatekeepers: Shallum, Akkub, Talmon, Ahiman and their brothers, Shallum their chief being stationed at the King's Gate on the east, up to the present time. These were the gatekeepers belonging to the camp of the Levites.* (1 Chronicles 9:16-17)

- *This Ezra went up from Babylon. He was a skilled scribe in the five books of Moses, which the Lord, the God of Israel, had given. And the king granted him all he asked, for the hand of the Lord his God was upon him.* (Ezra 7:6, AMPC)

- *Then Jeremiah called Baruch son of Neriah, and Baruch wrote upon the scroll of the book all the words which Jeremiah dictated, [words] that the Lord had spoken to him.* (Jeremiah 36:4, AMPC)

- *Then Daniel answered the king, "You may keep your gifts for yourself and give your rewards to someone else. Nevertheless, I will read the writing for the king and tell him what it means."* (Daniel 5:17)

- *He said to them, "Go into all the world and preach the good news to all creation."* (Mark 16:15)

- *Even on My servants, both men and women, I will pour out My Spirit in those days, and they will prophesy.* (Acts 2:18)

- *How, then, can they call on the one they have*

not believed in? And how can they believe in the one of whom they have not heard? And how can they hear without someone preaching to them? And how can they preach unless they are sent? As it is written, "How beautiful are the feet of those who bring good news!" (Romans 10:14-15)

- *Even though you have ten thousand guardians in Christ, you do not have many fathers, for in Christ Jesus I became your father through the gospel.* (1 Corinthians 4:14)

- *I know a man in Christ who fourteen years ago was caught up to the third heaven. Whether it was in the body or out of the body I do not know - God knows. And I know that this man - whether in the body or apart from the body I do not know, but God knows - was caught up to paradise. He heard inexpressible things, things that man is not permitted to tell.* (2 Corinthians 12:2-4)

- *I urge, then, first of all, that requests, prayers, intercession and thanksgiving be made for everyone - for kings and all those in authority, that we may live peaceful and quiet lives in all godliness and holiness.* (1 Timothy 2:1-2)

The functions of the church are special abilities mentioned in Scripture that are not classified as spiritual gifts, ministry offices, appointments, expressions, or attributes. They are a specific classification of spiritual abilities that help the church to function, helping to meet every need that exists. They are preachers, missionaries, dreamers and visionaries, interpreters of dreams and visions, intercessors, watchmen and gatekeepers, servants, scribes, spiritual parents, and mystics.

What is the fruit of the Spirit?

- *But the fruit of the Spirit is love, joy, peace, patience, kindness, goodness, faithfulness, gentleness and self-control. Against such things there is no law.* (Galatians 5:22-23)

The fruit of the Spirit is the product of the Holy Spirit's work within us over a long period of time. It is something that takes a great deal of work and effort on the Spirit's part to perfect within each of us. The fruit of the Spirit relates to the way we carry ourselves, interact with others, and our general personal disposition. This product manifests in love, joy, peace, patience, kindness, goodness, faithfulness, gentleness, and self-control. Nowhere in the world is there any prohibition on the development of such essential characteristics.

Why do we believe in unity?

- *How good and pleasant it is when brothers live together in unity!* (Psalm 133:1)

- *I in them and You in Me. May they be brought to complete unity to let the world know that you sent Me and have loved them even as you have loved Me.* (John 17:23)

- *So the churches were strengthened in the faith and grew daily in numbers.* (Acts 16:5)

- *May the God Who gives endurance and encouragement give you a spirit of unity among yourselves as you follow Christ Jesus.* (Romans 15:5)

- *I appeal to you, brothers, in the Name of our Lord Jesus Christ, that all of you agree with one another so that there may be no divisions among you and that you may be perfectly united in mind and thought.* (1 Corinthians 1:10)

- *Make every effort to keep the unity of the Spirit through the bond of peace.* (Ephesians 4:3)

- *Remember that at that time you were separate from Christ, excluded from citizenship in Israel and foreigners to the covenants of the promise, without hope and without God in the world. But now in Christ Jesus you who once were far away have been brought near through the blood of Christ…He came and preached peace to you who were far away and peace to those who were near.* (Ephesians 2:12-13,17)

- *And over all these virtues put on love, which binds them all together in perfect unity.* (Colossians 3:14)

Unity is a central theme in Scripture because God's work has always been accomplished through teamwork. As individuals come together, we value the concept of divine purpose and principle over the things we may not always like about someone else. We recognize the bond of peace comes through the work of the Spirit, which brings us to a place of unity. We cannot accomplish unity without the active work of the Spirit among our communities.

Why don't we discuss or promote politics?

- *The LORD had said to Abram, "Leave your country, your people and your father's household and go to the land I will show you. "I will make you into a great nation and I will bless you; I will make your name great, and you will be a blessing."* (Genesis 12:1-2)

- *For You singled them out from all the nations of the world to be Your own inheritance, just as you declared through your servant Moses when you, O Sovereign LORD, brought our fathers out of Egypt."* (1 Kings 8:53)

- *I will pour out My Spirit on all people…And everyone who calls on the Name of the Lord will be saved.* (Acts 2:17,21)

- *Love must be sincere. Hate what is evil; cling to what is good. Be devoted to one another in brotherly love. Honor one another above yourselves.* (Romans 12:9-10)

- *Therefore come out from them and be separate, says the Lord. Touch no unclean thing, and I will receive you.* (2 Corinthians 6:17)

- *Consequently, you are no longer foreigners and aliens, but fellow citizens with God's people and members of God's household…* (Ephesians 2:19)

- *That at the Name of Jesus every knee should bow, in heaven and on earth and under the earth, and every tongue confess that Jesus Christ is Lord, to the glory of God the Father.* (Philippians 2:10-11)

- *But our citizenship is in heaven. And we eagerly await a Savior from there, the Lord*

Jesus Christ... (Philippians 3:20)

- *And they sang a new song: "You are worthy to take the scroll and to open its seals, because You were slain, and with Your blood You purchased men for God from every tribe and language and people and nation."* (Revelation 5:9)

- *"We give thanks to You, Lord God Almighty, the One Who is and Who was, because You have taken Your great power and have begun to reign."* (Revelation 11:17)

Nationalism, as is understood in our modern times, is not a Biblical concept. God has called His people from every nation of this world to compose His Kingdom (or sphere of governance). Christians come from and are found in every tribe, tongue, and nation. Earthly politics set to divide, separate, and control. In the presence of Christ, every knee shall bow, and every earthly power shall one day fall. We prepare for this time as we love people with the love of Christ, regardless of their political background or affiliation. We respect differences of opinion and do not idolize any political system, government, or ideology.

Why do we talk about the Kingdom of God?

- *Your house and Your Kingdom will endure forever before me; Your throne will be established forever.* (2 Samuel 7:16)

- *For dominion belongs to the LORD and He rules over the nations.* (Psalm 22:28)

- *Your throne, O God, will last for ever and ever; a scepter of justice will be the scepter of Your Kingdom.* (Psalm 45:6)

- *The LORD has established His throne in heaven, and His kingdom rules over all.* (Psalm 103:19)

- *Repent, for the Kingdom of heaven is near.* (Matthew 3:2)

- *Blessed are those who are persecuted because of righteousness, for theirs is the Kingdom of heaven.* (Matthew 5:10)

- *But if I drive out demons by the Spirit of God, then the Kingdom of God has come upon you.* (Matthew 12:28)

- *After this, Jesus traveled about from one town and village to another, proclaiming the good news of the Kingdom of God.* (Luke 8:1)

- *Heal the sick who are there and tell them,*

'The Kingdom of God is near you.' (Luke 10:9)

- *And when He was demanded of the Pharisees, when the Kingdom of God should come, He answered them and said, The kingdom of God cometh not with observation: Neither shall they say, Lo here! or, lo there! for, behold, the Kingdom of God is within you.* (Luke 17:20-21, KJV)

- *Jesus said, "My Kingdom is not of this world. If it were, my servants would fight to prevent my arrest by the Jews. But now My Kingdom is from another place."* (John 18:36)

- *For the kingdom of God is not a matter of talk but of power.* (1 Corinthians 4:20)

We believe the Kingdom of God is the Kingdom of heaven come to earth, recognizing God's dominion as Lord of all in heaven and on earth. The Scriptures teach us the Kingdom of God is so near, one can reach out and touch it (it is "at hand," is near). We believe that God is the supreme ruler, even if it doesn't seem like it all the time. Here, in the church, the Kingdom of God becomes the meeting place of the Kingdom of heaven on earth. When we are part of the Kingdom of God, we accept God's divine rule in our lives and we live by His precepts, even when they don't line up with those found in the world. We know that as Kingdom citizens, we embody God's appointed precepts, leadership, and conduct, and as we walk and work together by the power of His

Spirit. The Kingdom of God works within us as we are born again, among us as through our fellowship, and around us, as we do His work.

Why do we believe there is only one faith?

- *And when they found them not, they drew Jason and certain brethren unto the rulers of the city, crying, These that have turned the world upside down are come hither also.* (Acts 17:6, KJV)

- *First, I thank my God through Jesus Christ for all of you, because your faith is being reported all over the world. God, Whom I serve with my whole heart in preaching the gospel of His Son, is my witness how constantly I remember you in my prayers at all times; and I pray that now at last by God's will the way may be opened for me to come to you. I long to see you so that I may impart to you some spiritual gift to make you strong-- that is, that you and I may be mutually encouraged by each other's faith.* (Romans 1:8-12)

- *For in the gospel a righteousness from God is revealed, a righteousness that is by faith from first to last, just as it is written: "The righteous will live by faith."* (Romans 1:17)

- *This righteousness from God comes through faith in Jesus Christ to all who believe.* (Romans 3:22)

- *To the Jews I became like a Jew, to win the Jews. To those under the law I became like one under the law (though I myself am not under the law), so as to win those under the law. To those not having the law I became like one not having the law (though I am not free from God's law but am under Christ's law), so as to win those not having the law. To the weak I became weak, to win the weak. I have become all things to all men so that by all possible means I might save some. I do all this for the sake of the gospel, that I may share in its blessings.* (1 Corinthians 9:20-23)

- *You show that you are a letter from Christ, the result of our ministry, written not with ink but with the Spirit of the living God, not on tablets of stone but on tablets of human hearts.* (2 Corinthians 3:3)

- *Therefore, since through God's mercy we have this ministry, we do not lose heart. Rather, we have renounced secret and shameful ways; we do not use deception, nor do we distort the word of God. On the contrary, by setting forth the truth plainly we commend ourselves to every man's conscience in the sight of God...For God, who said, "Let light shine out of darkness," made his light shine in our hearts to give us the light of the knowledge of the glory of God in the face of Christ. But we have this treasure in jars of clay to show that this all-surpassing power is from God and not from us.* (2 Corinthians 4:1-2,6-7)

- *...one Lord, one faith, one baptism...* (Ephesians 4:5)

There are many different religious systems in this world. Some have very noble ideas and promote positive values, but we do not believe all paths lead to God. We believe there is only one faith that unites us to God unto the end of salvation (redemption from sin). This is accomplished only in faith through Jesus Christ. We are saved by God's grace through faith. Our faith begins with repentance and confession, followed by baptism in water. Through our faith, we become a witness and a resource: inspired to become all things to all people. Our faith is so radical and changing, we turn the world upside down with it. It is radical because it starts with us and extends to others.

What is the church?

- *And I tell you that you are Peter, and on this rock I will build My church, and the gates of Hades will not overcome it.* (Matthew 16:18)

- *"If your brother sins against you, go and show him his fault, just between the two of you. If he listens to you, you have won your brother over. But if he will not listen, take one or two others along, so that 'every matter may be established by the testimony of two or three witnesses.' If he refuses to listen to them, tell it to the church; and if he refuses to listen even to the church, treat him as you would a pagan or a tax collector. "I tell you the truth, whatever you bind on earth will be bound in heaven, and whatever you loose on earth will be loosed in heaven. "Again, I tell you that if two of you on earth agree about anything you ask for, it will be done for you by My Father in heaven. For where two or three come together in My Name, there am I with them."* (Matthew 18:15-20)

- *Then the church throughout Judea, Galilee and Samaria enjoyed a time of peace. It was strengthened; and encouraged by the Holy Spirit, it grew in numbers, living in the fear of the Lord.* (Acts 9:31)

- *So Peter was kept in prison, but the church was earnestly praying to God for him.* (Acts 12:5)

- *When they came to Jerusalem, they were welcomed by the church and the apostles and elders, to whom they reported everything God had done through them.*

(Acts 15:4)

- *To the church of God in Corinth, to those
  sanctified in Christ Jesus and called to be
  holy, together with all those everywhere who
  call on the Name of our Lord Jesus Christ -
  their Lord and ours.* (1 Corinthians 1:2)

- *And in the church God has appointed first of
  all apostles, second prophets, third teachers,
  then workers of miracles, also those having
  gifts of healing, those able to help others,
  those with gifts of administration, and those
  speaking in different kinds of tongues.* (1
  Corinthians 12:28)

- *The churches in the province of Asia send you
  greetings. Aquila and Priscilla greet you
  warmly in the Lord, and so does the church
  that meets at their house.* (1 Corinthians
  16:19)

- *His intent was that now, through the church,
  the manifold wisdom of God should be made
  known to the rulers and authorities in the
  heavenly realms, according to His eternal
  purpose which He accomplished in Christ
  Jesus our Lord.* (Ephesians 3:10-11)

- *Let us hold unswervingly to the hope we
  profess, for He Who promised is faithful. And
  let us consider how we may spur one another
  on toward love and good deeds. Let us not*

give up meeting together, as some are in the habit of doing, but let us encourage one another - and all the more as you see the Day approaching. (Hebrews 10:23-25)

- *But you have come to Mount Zion, to the heavenly Jerusalem, the city of the living God. You have come to thousands upon thousands of angels in joyful assembly, to the church of the firstborn, whose names are written in heaven. You have come to God, the judge of all men, to the spirits of righteous men made perfect, to Jesus the mediator of a new covenant, and to the sprinkled blood that speaks a better word than the blood of Abel.* (Hebrews 12:22-24)

The word "church" means "called out" in the Greek. This meaning both defines the church and what the church is. It first means we are called out of the world into the Body of Christ (which is also a term used to define the church). This is a long-established pattern for the people of God: Noah, Abraham, Moses, the Prophets, and others throughout history were also "called" from among a larger group and established to do the work of God in their era. This signifies that God does something "new," against the standards of what is accepted, in every era of history. Its second meaning indicates what we are called to do: to an assembly, to a participation, to another group. It calls us out of what is comfortable for us in life; what is familiar and convenient, and assembles us with together with other believers, those who have made the same commitment. We are called, here and now, to be in the world, but not of the world. This is why we assemble and gather; it encourages us, edifies us, and ultimately helps us focus in a greater way than we can on our own.

The church is both local (local congregations or assemblies) and universal (international). The local church is part of the universal church, and the two work together to expand the Gospel, worldwide. The universal church is overseen by apostles and prophets, and the local church is overseen by pastors. Evangelists help reach those who are not born again and those who are away from the faith. Teachers can work either internationally or locally.

Jesus has promised the church will survive through to the end of the time, as God's people active and working in this era of history. It shall never be overcome, even when it fights the enemy in all its forms. We, therefore, make every effort to let the Spirit work through us to avoid internal conflicts that also can cause the church to suffer damage. Instead, we seek to edify and build one another up in love. We receive correction when necessary and we do things within divine order, so as to cause offense to none.

What is the body of Christ?

- *Now the body is not made up of one part but*

of many... But in fact God has arranged the parts in the body, every one of them, just as he wanted them to be...As it is, there are many parts, but one body. (1 Corinthians 12:14,18,20)

- *Now you are the body of Christ, and each one of you is a part of it.* (1 Corinthians 12:27)

- *For He Himself is our peace, Who has made the two one and has destroyed the barrier, the dividing wall of hostility, by abolishing in His flesh the law with its commandments and regulations. His purpose was to create in Himself one new man out of the two, thus making peace, and in this one body to reconcile both of them to God through the cross, by which He put to death their hostility.* (Ephesians 2:14-16)

- *There is one body...* (Ephesians 4:4)

- *Therefore each of you must put off falsehood and speak truthfully to his neighbor, for we are all members of one body.* (Ephesians 4:25)

- *After all, no one ever hated his own body, but he feeds and cares for it, just as Christ does the church - for we are members of His body.* (Ephesians 5:29-30)

- *Let the peace of Christ rule in your hearts,*

since as members of one body you were called to peace. And be thankful. (Colossians 3:15)

The Scriptures teach us the body of Christ is another term for the church. The head of the Church is Christ Jesus Himself. Those who follow Him are part of His body as He leads us: He leads as we study His teaching, as we follow the leaders He has provide, and as we follow all of this through the guidance and direction of His Spirit. The Body of Christ is known by many different terms: The Kingdom of God, the Kingdom, the Bride of Christ, the assembly, the Way, Saints, the Lamb's wife, the Family in Heaven and on Earth, God's building, God's garden, the Habitation of God, Heavenly Jerusalem, His flock, Holy City, House of God, Household of Faith, Israel of God, Pillar and Ground of Truth, Spiritual House, Temple of God, Tabernacle, and Sanctuary (holy place).

Why do we believe there is only one body of Christ?

- *My prayer is not that You take them out of the world but that You protect them from the evil one. They are not of the world, even as I am not of it. Sanctify them by the truth; Your Word is truth. As You sent Me into the world, I have sent them into the world. For them I sanctify myself, that they too may be truly sanctified…I have given them the glory that*

You gave Me, that they may be one as We are one: I in them and you in Me. May they be brought to complete unity to let the world know that You sent Me and have loved them even as You have loved Me. (Acts 17:15-19,22-23)

- *Be completely humble and gentle; be patient, bearing with one another in love...There is one body...* (Ephesians 4:2,4)

- *So, my brothers, you also died to the law through the body of Christ, that you might belong to another, to Him Who was raised from the dead, in order that we might bear fruit to God.* (Romans 7:4)

- *The body is a unit, though it is made up of many parts; and though all its parts are many, they form one body. So it is with Christ... Now you are the body of Christ, and each one of you is a part of it.* (1 Corinthians 12:12,27)

- *Let the peace of Christ rule in your hearts, since as members of one body you were called to peace. And be thankful.* (Colossians 3:15)

The church is a real and living entity spread throughout the entire world. It is not bound by one specific rule or denomination, but by the living spiritual experience had by God's people following His Spirit. The church does not consist of just one ethnic group, but all; not just one type of person, but many. We are not bound by race, sex, origins, sexuality, orientation, politics, social status, or other divisions that separate human beings on this planet. All come before Christ as both victims of sin and perpetrators of it. We find our ultimate promise and redemption in Christ, rather than the aspirations of this world. As a result, we all come to the Kingdom: we all give, we all worship, we all share in our gifts and the gifts of others, and all of us participate.

Why do we practice communion?

- *While they were eating, Jesus took bread, gave thanks and broke it, and gave it to His disciples, saying, "Take and eat; this is My Body." Then He took the cup, gave thanks and offered it to them, saying, "Drink from it, all of you. This is My Blood of the covenant, which is poured out for many for the forgiveness of sins. I tell you, I will not drink of this fruit of the vine from now on until that day when I drink it anew with you in My Father's Kingdom." When they had sung a hymn, they went out to the Mount of Olives.* (Matthew 26:26-30)

- *While they were eating, Jesus took bread, gave thanks and broke it, and gave it to His disciples, saying, "Take it; this is My body."*

Then He took the cup, gave thanks and offered it to them, and they all drank from it. "This is My Blood of the covenant, which is poured out for many," He said to them. "I tell you the truth, I will not drink again of the fruit of the vine until that day when I drink it anew in the Kingdom of God." When they had sung a hymn, they went out to the Mount of Olives. (Mark 14:22-26)

- *After taking the cup, He gave thanks and said, "Take this and divide it among you. For I tell you I will not drink again of the fruit of the vine until the Kingdom of God comes." And He took bread, gave thanks and broke it, and gave it to them, saying, "This is My Body given for you; do this in remembrance of Me." In the same way, after the supper he took the cup, saying, "This cup is the new covenant in My Blood, which is poured out for you.* (Luke 22:17-20)

- *Is not the cup of thanksgiving for which we give thanks a participation in the blood of Christ? And is not the bread that we break a participation in the body of Christ? Because there is one loaf, we, who are many, are one body, for we all partake of the one loaf.* (1 Corinthians 10:16-17)

- *For I received from the Lord what I also passed on to you: The Lord Jesus, on the night He was betrayed, took bread, and when*

He had given thanks, He broke it and said, "This is My Body, which is for you; do this in remembrance of Me." In the same way, after supper He took the cup, saying, "This cup is the new covenant in My Blood; do this, whenever you drink it, in remembrance of me." For whenever you eat this bread and drink this cup, you proclaim the Lord's death until He comes. (1 Corinthians 11:23-26)

Communion (also called Holy Communion, the Lord's Supper, or the Love Feast) is a special ordinance of the Lord instituted the night before He died (during the annual Passover dinner). It symbolizes the way in which Christ gave Himself for us, both body and blood, on the cross. The unleavened bread used symbolizes His body, and the wine (fruit of the vine) symbolizes His blood. When we partake of communion, we do so in memory of the sacrifice Christ made for us. It symbolizes our union with Christ and our union with one another in His Body. We practice communion because it brings us closer to God and closer into communion with His believers (the church). At Sanctuary, we do this as often as we can usually when we gather on Sundays.

Who do we believe is welcome at the communion table?

- *Therefore, whoever eats the bread or drinks the cup of the Lord in an unworthy manner will be guilty of sinning against the body and blood of the Lord. A man ought to examine himself before he eats of the bread and drinks of the cup. For anyone who eats and drinks without recognizing the body of the Lord eats and drinks judgment on himself. That is why many among you are weak and sick, and a number of you have fallen asleep.* (1 Corinthians 11:27-31)

We believe it is essential for every believer to examine their own conscience before receiving communion. Such is a personal examination, one between an individual and God. Anyone who desires to receive is welcome to do so at Sanctuary. Communion consists of unleavened bread and unfermented grape juice when communion is practiced in-house, during church service. When we are at a dinner or some outside occasion, informal communion may use any bread or beverage available, echoing the fact that Jesus used what was most available and accessible to Him to teach an important spiritual lesson (what was already on the table). We do not use alcohol in our communion services to enable all to partake, including those who may be sensitive to alcohol due to allergy, medication, or those in active recovery. Children who are able to safely consume communion items are welcome to partake, as well.

What do we believe an apostolic fellowship looks like?

- *Those who accepted his message were baptized, and about three thousand were added to their number that day. They devoted themselves to the apostles' teaching and to the fellowship, to the breaking of bread and to prayer. Everyone was filled with awe, and many wonders and miraculous signs were done by the apostles. All the believers were together and had everything in common. Selling their possessions and goods, they gave to anyone as he had need. Every day they continued to meet together in the temple courts. They broke bread in their homes and ate together with glad and sincere hearts, praising God and enjoying the favor of all the people. And the Lord added to their number daily those who were being saved. (Acts 2:41-47)*

- *For this reason I kneel before the Father, from Whom His whole family in heaven and on earth derives its name. I pray that out of His glorious riches He may strengthen you with power through His Spirit in your inner being, so that Christ may dwell in your hearts through faith. And I pray that you, being rooted and established in love, may have power, together with all the saints, to grasp how wide and long and high and deep is the love of Christ, and to know this love that surpasses knowledge--that you may be filled to the measure of all the fullness of God. Now to Him Who is able to do immeasurably more than all we ask or imagine, according to His power that is at work within us, to Him be glory in the church and in Christ Jesus throughout all generations, for ever and ever! Amen.* (Ephesians 3:14-21)

- *We proclaim to you what we have seen and heard, so that you also may have fellowship with us. And our fellowship is with the Father and with His Son, Jesus Christ…But if we walk in the light, as He is in the light, we have fellowship with one another, and the blood of Jesus, His Son, purifies us from all sin.* (1 John 1:3,7)

We believe apostolic fellowship looks like the first century church, applied within a modern construct for our day and time. The early apostolic community was united by a common bond of experience: they came together, having heard the word, believed it, were baptized, and united under the teaching of the apostles. They gathered together in homes, in assemblies, wherever they were able to do so, in order to share spiritual identity and life with one another. That is the essence of their work: because they were believers, they became a part of something new and different beyond what they experienced before. They became family: they worshiped together, prayed together, studied Scripture together, shared about God together, shared in meals together, had communion together, and gave together. They were more than a church; they were a faith family, one bound by spiritual experience.

What is a "life worthy of the calling we have received?"

- *As a prisoner for the Lord, then, I urge you to live a life worthy of the calling you have received.* (Ephesians 4:1)

- *Your Kingdom come, Your will be done on earth as it is in heaven. Give us today our daily bread. Forgive us our debts, as we also have forgiven our debtors. And lead us not into temptation, but deliver us from the evil one.* (Matthew 6:10-13)

- *But seek first His Kingdom and His righteousness, and all these things will be given to you as well.* (Matthew 6:33)

- *Therefore, whoever humbles himself like this child is the greatest in the Kingdom of heaven.* (Matthew 18:4)

- *For the Kingdom of God is not a matter of eating and drinking, but of righteousness, peace and joy in the Holy Spirit.* (Romans 14:17)

- *For the Kingdom of God is not a matter of talk but of power.* (1 Corinthians 4:20)

- *Therefore, if anyone is in Christ, he is a new creation; the old has gone, the new has come!* (2 Corinthians 5:17)

- *But you are a chosen people, a royal priesthood, a holy nation, a people belonging to God, that you may declare the praises of Him Who called you out of darkness into His wonderful light. Once you were not a people, but now you are the people of God; once you had not received mercy, but now you have received mercy.* (1 Peter 2:9-10)

As Christians, we recognize our first calling is to God because we are now "citizens of heaven." We are a new people! We believe this means our first duty is to God's work, to seek first God, and His righteousness, and all that we need shall be added unto us. For this reason, we promote, proclaim, and share this great work through the Gospel to all who shall listen.

Why do we believe in giving?

- *All who cross over, those twenty years old or more, are to give an offering to the LORD.* (Exodus 30:14)

- *A tithe of everything from the land, whether grain from the soil or fruit from the trees, belongs to the LORD; it is holy to the LORD.* (Leviticus 27:30)

- *Speak to the Levites and say to them: 'When you receive from the Israelites the tithe I give you as your inheritance, you must present a tenth of that tithe as the LORD's offering."* (Numbers 18:26)

- *Bring the whole tithe into the storehouse, that there may be food in my house. Test Me in this," says the LORD Almighty, "and see if I will not throw open the floodgates of heaven and pour out so much blessing that you will not have room enough for it."* (Malachi 3:10)

- *"Do not store up for yourselves treasures on earth, where moth and rust destroy, and where thieves break in and steal. But store up for yourselves treasures in heaven, where moth and rust do not destroy, and where thieves do not break in and steal. For where your treasure is, there your heart will be also."* (Matthew 6:19-20)

- *Give, and it will be given to you. A good measure, pressed down, shaken together and running over, will be poured into your lap. For with the measure you use, it will be measured to you.* (Luke 6:38)

- *As He looked up, Jesus saw the rich putting their gifts into the temple treasury. He also saw a poor widow put in two very small copper coins. "I tell you the truth," He said, "this poor widow has put in more than all the others. All these people gave their gifts out of their wealth; but she out of her poverty put in all she had to live on."* (Luke 21:1-4)

- *In everything I did, I showed you that by this kind of hard work we must help the weak, remembering the words the Lord Jesus Himself said: 'It is more blessed to give than to receive.'* (Acts 20:35)

- *Therefore, I urge you, brothers, in view of God's mercy, to offer your bodies as living sacrifices, holy and pleasing to God - this is your spiritual act of worship.* (Romans 12:1)

- *And here is my advice about what is best for you in this matter: Last year you were the first not only to give but also to have the desire to do so.* (2 Corinthians 8:10)

- *Each man should give what he has decided in his heart to give, not reluctantly or under compulsion, for God loves a cheerful giver.* (2 Corinthians 9:7)

Giving is an intimate and essential part of the Christian life. We give because God gave to us first, through Jesus Christ. Rather than give something random, God gave of Himself. We, too, give of ourselves. We recognize giving in all its forms: that it begins with tithing, the offering of 10% of one's profit or income, as an initial tool. We know that tithing is used to help teach us about giving, but it is not where giving ends. We know we are called to give what we can, from what we have, above and beyond what may be required for us to do so. We give from what we have, so the Kingdom of God can continue and advance.

We also do not believe giving is just financial, but an attitude. We give of our finances; we give of our time for the growth and continuation of God's work (serving and volunteering); we give to those in need; and we give of ourselves, as an acceptable offering for God's service. We offer all that we are and all that we have for His glory, in His grace.

What do we believe is the one hope to which we are called?

- *There is one body and one Spirit - just as you*

were called to one hope when you were called. *(Ephesians 4:4)*

- *And I am confident in the Lord that I myself will come soon.* (Philippians 2:24)

- *Brothers, we do not want you to be ignorant about those who fall asleep, or to grieve like the rest of men, who have no hope. We believe that Jesus died and rose again and so we believe that God will bring with Jesus those who have fallen asleep in Him. According to the Lord's own word, we tell you that we who are still alive, who are left till the coming of the Lord, will certainly not precede those who have fallen asleep. For the Lord Himself will come down from heaven, with a loud command, with the voice of the archangel and with the trumpet call of God, and the dead in Christ will rise first. After that, we who are still alive and are left will be caught up together with them in the clouds to meet the Lord in the air. And so we will be with the Lord forever. Therefore encourage each other with these words.* (1 Thessalonians 4:13-18)

- *While we wait for the blessed hope--the glorious appearing of our great God and Savior, Jesus Christ, Who gave Himself for us to redeem us from all wickedness and to purify for Himself a people that are His very own, eager to do what is good.* (Titus 2:13)

- *...so Christ was sacrificed once to take away the sins of many people; and He will appear a second time, not to bear sin, but to bring salvation to those who are waiting for Him.* (Hebrews 9:28)

- *But the day of the Lord will come like a thief. The heavens will disappear with a roar; the elements will be destroyed by fire, and the earth and everything in it will be laid bare.* (2 Peter 3:10)

- *And now, dear children, continue in Him, so that when He appears we may be confident and unashamed before Him at His coming.* (1 John 2:28)

- *He who testifies to these things says, "Yes, I am coming soon." Amen. Come, Lord Jesus.* (Revelation 2:20)

We do not have a full picture of everything that will happen after Jesus Christ returns. Instead, we have pictures and pieces of what it will be like, to inspire us in truth and hope. Jesus Christ has always remained faithful to His promises: He died, rose from the dead, and shall come again. This is the hope to which we are called: the promise of seeing the Kingdom of God in its full establishment throughout the world. No longer shall we battle with sin's effects, but shall instead, experience a true union between heaven and earth, where God reigns supreme, not just in a general sense, but over the heart of each person.

Why do we believe in the Scriptures?

- *And He began by saying to them, "Today this Scripture is fulfilled in your hearing." (Luke 4:21)*

- *And beginning with Moses and all the Prophets, He explained to them what was said in all the Scriptures concerning Himself. (Luke 24:27)*

- *After He was raised from the dead, His disciples recalled what He had said. Then they believed the Scripture and the words that Jesus had spoken. (John 2:22)*

- *These things happened so that the Scripture would be fulfilled... (John 19:36)*

- *What does the Scripture say? (Romans 4:3)*

- *Until I come, devote yourself to the public reading of Scripture, to preaching and to teaching. (1 Timothy 4:13)*

- *But as for you, continue in what you have learned and have become convinced of, because you know those from whom you learned it, and how from infancy you have known the holy Scriptures, which are able to make you wise for salvation through faith in Christ Jesus. All Scripture is God-breathed and is useful for teaching, rebuking, correcting and training in righteousness, so that the man of God may be thoroughly equipped for every good work.* (2 Timothy 3:14-17)

- *If you really keep the royal law found in Scripture, "Love your neighbor as yourself," you are doing right.* (James 2:8)

- *Above all, you must understand that no prophecy of Scripture came about by the prophet's own interpretation.* (2 Peter 1:20)

We believe the Scriptures are the written word of God. These writings are the word of God because they are inspired experiences, songs, poems, histories, writings, stories, accounts, letters, and statements that individuals were divinely led to document throughout history. Scripture doesn't stand to answer every single issue human beings may have. Because it contains differing accounts, there may be parts of it that don't always make sense to us right now or might not always seem to agree with each other. This is not because Scripture isn't true to its revelation, but because not every situation accounts for the same response all the time. Scripture shows us God has been with humanity from the beginning and that God has had a plan for salvation (uniting us with Him) since the very beginning. When we study Scripture, we learn about God, we learn about the ways His people have succeeded and failed throughout history, and we find the ultimate hope for ourselves.

At Sanctuary, we use the Bible as is understood to be used within the western canon. We also, at times, will use or reference works that are part of other Biblical canons around the world or other historical works, but are not included in western canonical reference. If you have any questions about what we use, please feel free to ask!

What is *Logos*?

- *The centurion replied, "Lord, I do not deserve to have You come under my roof. But just say the word, and my servant will be healed."* (Matthew 8:8)

- *When anyone hears the message about the Kingdom and does not understand it, the evil one comes and snatches away what was sown in his heart. This is the seed sown along the path. The one who received the seed that fell on rocky places is the man who hears the word and at once receives it with joy. But since he has no root, he lasts only a short time. When trouble or persecution comes because of the word, he quickly falls away.*

The one who received the seed that fell among the thorns is the man who hears the word, but the worries of this life and the deceitfulness of wealth choke it, making it unfruitful. But the one who received the seed that fell on good soil is the man who hears the word and understands it. He produces a crop, yielding a hundred, sixty or thirty times what was sown. (Matthew 13:19-23)

- *...just as they were handed down to us by those who from the first were eyewitnesses and servants of the word.* (Luke 1:2)

- *He replied, "Blessed rather are those who hear the word of God and obey it."* (Luke 11:28)

- *In the beginning was the Word, and the Word was with God, and the Word was God...The Word became flesh and made His dwelling among us. We have seen His glory, the glory of the One and Only, Who came from the Father, full of grace and truth.* (John 1:1,14)

- *I tell you the truth, if anyone keeps My word, he will never see death."* (John 8:51)

- *After they prayed, the place where they were meeting was shaken. And they were all filled with the Holy Spirit and spoke the word of God boldly.* (Acts 4:31)

- *The word of the Lord spread through the whole region.* (Acts 13:49)

- *To one there is given through the Spirit the message of wisdom, to another the message of knowledge by means of the same Spirit...* (1 Corinthians 12:8)

- *For the word of God is living and active. Sharper than any double-edged sword, it penetrates even to dividing soul and spirit, joints and marrow; it judges the thoughts and attitudes of the heart.* (Hebrews 4:12)

There is more than one Greek term translated as "word" in the English. Each one of these terms holds within it a different meaning. As a result, we don't always recognize, nor understand their meanings when we read Scripture in English translations. One of these terms is the Greek word for "*logos.*" *Logos,* translated as "word," means much, much more than just "word" in the way we understand it in English. *Logos* is a Greek concept of understanding, revelation, and precept that relates to the implementation of divine order within a situation.

<u>**Why do we believe it is important to create a solid foundation in Scriptural and revelatory instruction?**</u>

- *Remember the day you stood before the LORD your God at Horeb, when He said to* me, *"Assemble the people before Me to hear My words so that they may learn to revere Me as long as they live in the land and may teach them to their children."* (Deuteronomy 4:10)

- *Not only was the Teacher wise, but also he imparted knowledge to the people. He pondered and searched out and set in order many proverbs. The Teacher searched to find just the right words, and what he wrote was upright and true.* (Ecclesiastes 12:9-10)

- *"Who is it he is trying to teach? To whom is he explaining his message? To children weaned from their milk, to those just taken from the breast? For it is: Do and do, do and do, rule on rule, rule on rule; a little here, a little there."* (Isaiah 28:9-10)

- *...but now revealed and made known through the prophetic writings by the command of the eternal God, so that all nations might believe and obey Him* (Romans 16:26)

- *Do your best to present yourself to God as one approved, a workman who does not need to be ashamed and who correctly handles the word of truth.* (2 Timothy 2:15)

We recognize both Scripture and *logos* require understanding. One of the reasons many err in interpretation and lack clarity in Scripture and divine direction is because they lack the essential understanding required to recognize the truth in Scripture and divine revelation. We cannot understand the ways of God without instruction. We cannot see the truth if we do not see how God reveals things to us: we see our knowledge in experience as God reveals to us through such things; the essential nature that for something to exist, God must first create it. To discover our true purpose, such must be revealed to those who exist. *Logos* manifests to us verbally through spiritual gifts; through divine teaching; and as God speaks to each and every one of us in ways only He can.

Why do we identify ourselves as a "belonging congregation?"

- *...to them I will give within My temple and its walls a memorial and a name better than sons and daughters; I will give them an everlasting name that will not be cut off. And foreigners who bind themselves to the LORD to serve Him, to love the Name of the LORD, and to worship Him, all who keep the Sabbath without desecrating it and who hold fast to My covenant - these I will bring to My holy mountain and give them joy in My house of prayer. Their burnt offerings and sacrifices will be accepted on my altar; for My house will be called a house of prayer for all nations.*

(Isaiah 56:5-7)

- *The LORD appeared to us in the past, saying: "I have loved you with an everlasting love; I have drawn you with loving-kindness. (Jeremiah 31:3)*

- *"This is what the LORD Almighty says: 'In a little while I will once more shake the heavens and the earth, the sea and the dry land. I will shake all nations, and the desired of all nations will come, and I will fill this house with glory,' says the LORD Almighty. 'The silver is mine and the gold is mine,' declares the LORD Almighty. 'The glory of this present house will be greater than the glory of the former house,' says the LORD Almighty. 'And in this place I will grant peace,' declares the LORD Almighty." (Haggai 2:6-9)*

- *Do not judge, or you too will be judged. For in the same way you judge others, you will be judged, and with the measure you use, it will be measured to you... Ask and it will be given to you; seek and you will find; knock and the door will be opened to you. For everyone who asks receives; he who seeks finds; and to him who knocks, the door will be opened. (Matthew 7:1-2,7-8)*

- *All that the Father gives Me will come to Me, and whoever comes to Me I will never drive away. (John 6:37)*

- *For God does not show favoritism.* (Romans 2:11)

- *Accept him whose faith is weak, without passing judgment on disputable matters. One man's faith allows him to eat everything, but another man, whose faith is weak, eats only vegetables. The man who eats everything must not look down on him who does not, and the man who does not eat everything must not condemn the man who does, for God has accepted him. Who are you to judge someone else's servant? To his own master he stands or falls. And he will stand, for the Lord is able to make him stand.* (Romans 14:1-4)

- *Accept one another, then, just as Christ accepted you, in order to bring praise to God.* (Romans 15:17)

- *The Spirit and the bride say, "Come!" And let him who hears say, "Come!" Whoever is thirsty, let him come; and whoever wishes, let him take the free gift of the water of life.* (Revelation 22:17)

We believe the house of God, the church, the Body of Christ, is for any and all who seek to know God. We walk in the principle of inclusion: that God calls "whosoever," and "whosoever comes is welcome. We do not believe in establishing limits upon who should, or shouldn't, come into God's house. We welcome every nationality, race, gender, sexual orientation, age, culture, marital status, language, minority, refugee, immigrant, family situation, or circumstance. We identify as more than just "inclusive," however. We identify as "belonging:" because in saying you are welcome, without condition, we affirm that you, as you are, have every right to know God, to follow His precepts, and belong here, with us, no matter who you are. At Sanctuary, we are more than just an institution. We are found family, a group of believers who, much like the early church, has become "found family" in a hostile world that doesn't always understand who we are. Our acceptance is here. Our love is here. Our place is here with God and our spiritual family.

OUR LOGO

The Sanctuary logo features a number of important themes that are essential to our spiritual work and our mission.

- **Four quadrants:** The four quadrants are divided up to represent four essential aspects of our spiritual instruction and development. Quadrant 1 represents our worship, prayer, and exercise of spiritual gifts. Quadrant 2 represents our commission to work in the world, moving in the unity of the Spirit and proclaiming the work of the Alpha and Omega, Jesus Christ, the beginning and the end. Quadrant 3 represents service (ministry) that starts with answering our baptismal call; and quadrant four represents our study of Scripture, bound by our communion, connection to the vine, and call to stand as the light of the world.

- **Quadrant 1**

  - **Hands open with radiance extending:** Our worship, praise, and prayer are central to our spiritual experience with God. We discover God in praise; we love God in our worship; we meet God in our prayer. These three form a powerful means by which we discover our spiritual gifts, present through the work of the Holy Spirit (Holy Ghost).

  - **Flame:** representative of the Holy Spirit (Ghost) at work within each and every one of us. We come to discover the power of the Spirit as we worship, praise, and pray.

- **Quadrant 2**

  - **Globe:** In the globe, we see two very important things about the nature of the church. First, the international nature of the church, composed of people from every tongue and tribe who come to call on the Name of the

Lord. Second, our commitment to the Great Commission, to be completed with our participation as we proclaim the Gospel to the world. By being a Christian, we are part of the most exciting work ever done in history.

- **White dove:** The dove has long been a representation of the Holy Spirit (Ghost). Here, the dove is seen carrying an olive branch. At Sanctuary, we are committed to maintaining the unity of the Spirit through the bond of peace. It is the Spirit that brings the promise of peace to the world and offers the true unity the church seeks.

- **Rainbow:** We chose the rainbow because it is a powerful symbol of covenant, revolution, and diversity as has been used throughout history. In modern times, the rainbow is often associated with the LGBTQ+ community, and by extension, to represent diversity and difference in people. We use it for these same purposes, and we also use it to echo the promise of God's covenant with humanity throughout history. The second covenant ever made in history (after the promised covenant to send the Messiah in Genesis 3) was with Noah, and the rainbow stands as a symbol of God's promise to never flood the earth again. God promised to look upon humanity and to institute times and seasons, seedtime, and harvest, for as long as earth remained. In the rainbow, we find a symbol of God's grace. Every time the rainbow appears in the sky, it proves we have a God Who loves us and Who cares about each and every one of us. He has created us differently, but He loves us all with the same powerful and abiding love that can only come from above.

The rainbow has been used throughout history as a sign of revolution and impending change. It was used by Reformationists in the sixteenth century during the German Peasants' War, is a sign of peace in Italy, as an LGBTQ+ social symbol, for the Rainbow Coalition (which stood against conservative politics which were exclusionary and encouraged separatism rather than diversity), in South Africa as a symbol of post-apartheid, and for various other social movements since the 1970s. We use it in this same tradition, proving diversity is first spiritual, and then social; and that by doing so, we welcome and embrace people of all backgrounds to worship with us, find refuge and safety, and the love of God here in this place.

- o **Alpha and Omega:** The Bible tells us that Jesus is the "Alpha and Omega." Jesus is literally the first and the last, the beginning and the end. He has been from the beginning, and will be forever, even in the end. This eloquent identity for Christ reveals His divine nature; His omnipresence; and omnipotence over the cosmos. His governance is eternal, without end, even over this world.

- **Quadrant 3**

  - o **Foot washing:** At the Last Supper, Jesus washed the feet of His disciples. After doing such, the disciples were told to do likewise. This powerful display of servanthood teaches us how we are to minister to the world: as servants, doing the work that needs to be done, even if no one else desires to do it.

  - o **Shell with water drop:** The shell with a drop of water signifies our baptism. In baptism, we die to ourselves in Christ and rise to new life. It is the foundation by which we discover who God calls us to be and how we can best serve in the Kingdom.

- <u>Quadrant 4</u>

  - **Open Bible:** Our commitment to studying Scripture gives us the ability to learn more about God. This education is not just in an ancient or intangible sense, but in one that helps us to develop faith and spiritual understanding for today. As we study Scripture, we develop a greater understanding of God's presence, God's work with humanity, and just how much God loves us, despite ourselves.

  - **Wheat stalk:** Bread, made from wheat, is found throughout the Bible. It symbolizes the sacrifice of Christ in communion, the unity of the church, the satisfaction of spiritual hunger, and our deep, sincere longing to be one with God, our Father.

  - **Grape bunch:** Grapes are used throughout the Bible to signify spiritual bounty, fruition, pressing, and calling. Grapes, used to make wine, also represent the shed blood of Christ for our redemption and the

New Covenant. That New Covenant is a new agreement with God, bound by grace rather than the law.

  o **Candle:** Jesus Christ is the light of the world. He illuminates our lives: our study, our vision, our path, and our future. As He lives within us, we too stand as His light in this world, representing Him wherever we go.

- **Center cross with compass point arrows and center heart:** The cross is the center of our faith. It symbolizes Christ's work for us on the cross, His sacrifice, and our redemption. Because of the cross, we have learned how to love others. We show that love in our work, in our ministries, and in our very lives. God's love has become ours, and it is our pleasure to share it with the world.

  The arrows on the cross remind us of our call to go: go into all the world, go and do something good for someone else, go and make a difference in someone's life, and go and grow. The love of God does not leave us still or static, but requires us to do something with the deposit of faith we now have through Jesus Christ.

- **Black circle:** Black represents our exterior lives: the flesh, the part of us that wars the temptation to sin against God. We don't always find ourselves on the winning side of that battle (even after salvation), which means the flesh reminds us, as it is, just how much we need God's grace to make it through this life. Black is used to display the nature of things that go along with it, and the fact that sometimes those things tempt us the most: the hope of power, influence, and strength, all of which means nothing if we do not have God.

- **Name of ministry:** Our name, Sanctuary International Fellowship Tabernacle, appears on our outer black circle in light green (green representing life). Our ministry name is our representation to the world. In our name, we show that we are an international, welcoming refuge; a fellowship of believers, more than friends, but truly family; and a tabernacle, or dwelling place, for God and worship. The light shows on the black, on the outer representation we carry, displaying that light, and spiritual life, always shine in darkness.

- **Red circle:** Red represents Blood of Christ, which changes our entire outlook and experience as human beings. The blood is our pathway to forgiveness as in it we find the change between the outer person and the inner person.

- **Words on red circle:** The words on the red

circle, the circle that divides our past and present and opens the door for our transformed nature, are the pillars of Sanctuary's purpose and call. They are: Grace, Renewal, Unity, Ministry, Hope, Faith, and Love.

- **White circle:** The white circle represents what the Bible calls the "inner man." The inner person is us, ourselves, transformed by Christ's work and brought into a new spiritual state. We can only come to find the essence of who we are if we find Christ. There, within the inner person, we find our heart of worship, spiritual gifts, communion, study, light, service, identity, calling, spirituality, and global impact.

- **Black ribbon:** The black ribbon holds everything together. We find our grounding when we are willing to come together, as we are, to be transformed by Jesus Christ. On it, in white lettering, we find the first half of our theme verse (2 Corinthians 4:7) and the establishment year of Sanctuary (2013). We know we are imperfect, but we offer ourselves, as we are, for God's service. If we come together and allow God to work in us, we can change ourselves, our world, and the world at large through the grace of God.

STATEMENT OF FAITH

- **We believe in one God:** the Father (spiritual parent) in creation, the Son in redemption, and the Holy Spirit as God in us, God with us, and God transforming us, in sanctification and experience. God is over all, through all, and in all (Genesis 1:1,26, Genesis 3:22, Exodus 3;14, Deuteronomy 6:4, Deuteronomy 32:18, Psalm 68:5, Isaiah 66:13, Hosea 11:3-4, Matthew 1:18-24, Matthew 3:11, Matthew 23:37, Luke 2:21, John 4:24, John 14:15-17, Acts 1:1-11, Acts 2:1-38, Ephesians 4:6, 1 John 5:7-8, Revelation 1:5-6).

- **We believe in one Lord, Jesus Christ:** the Only Begotten of the Father, born of a virgin, conceived of the Holy Spirit, crucified, died, raised from the grave, and was the very Word made flesh and Image of the invisible God, the Name by which men may be saved (Isaiah 9:6, Matthew 1:18-24, John 1:1-18, John 10:17, John 14:6, John 15:13, John 20:1-31, Acts 4:12, Ephesians 4:5, Philippians 2:10, Colossians 1:15-23, Hebrews 4:14-15, 1 John 3:16, Revelation 5:9-13).

- **We believe in one Spirit, the Holy Spirit, Who dwells within us:** manifesting the evidence of spiritual gifts, the Ephesians 4:11 leadership gifts, the appointment works, gifting attributes, prophetic expressions, functions, and the Spirit's unique fruit, guiding us, leading us, and bringing us to a full experience with God (Genesis 18:16-33, Genesis 40:1-23, Exodus 25:18-22, Exodus 35:20-35, Deuteronomy 31:19-22, 2 Samuel 6:14, 2 Samuel 18:24-33, 2 Samuel 21:10-15, 2 Kings 17:24-41, 1 Chronicles 16:41-42, 1 Chronicles 9:8-34, 2 Chronicles 5;12-14, Ezra 7:6, Job 33:4, Psalm 45:1, Psalm 149:3, Psalm 150:4, Isaiah 11:2-5, Isaiah 29:16, Ezekiel 12:1-11, Jeremiah 36:1-32, Daniel 5:1-31, Matthew 3:11, Matthew 23:34, Mark 16:15-20, John 20:22, Acts 1:5,8, Acts 2:14-21,38, Acts 6:3-6, Romans 8:14-17, Romans 8:28, Romans 10:5-18, Romans 12:4-10, 1 Corinthians 12:1-28, 2 Corinthians 12:1-10, Galatians 5:22-33, Ephesians 2:19-20, Ephesians 4:4,11-16, Philippians 1:1, 1 Timothy 2:1-7, 1 Timothy 3:1-8, 1 Timothy 5:17, Titus 1:5-7, Titus 2:3-8, Hebrews 7:25, 1 Peter 5:1, Jude 1:3, Revelation 4:4, Revelation 18:20, Revelation 19:10, Revelation 21:1-22:11).

- **We believe in the unity of the Spirit present through the bond of peace:** the peace of the Kingdom must be maintained at all costs. Anything that causes dissention, hostility, or worldly attitudes (such as worldly politics) must cease in the presence of God's true Kingdom. As such, we do not believe politics or worldly social structures of any sort have place in the church, and should not be employed therein (Genesis 12:1-20, 1 Kings 8:53, Psalm 133:1, John 17:23, Acts 2:17-21, Acts 16:5, Romans 15:5, 1 Corinthians 1:10, 2 Corinthians 6:17, Ephesians 2:12-22, Ephesians 4:3, Philippians 2:10-11, Philippians 3:17-21, Colossians 3:14, Revelation 5:9, Revelation 18:4).

- **We believe there is one faith:** we are saved by God's grace through faith. Our faith begins with our repentance and confession, as we are spiritually transformed. Our faith leads us to stand as both a witness and a resource, following the inspiration of the apostolic work to become all things to all people. It is our honor to turn the world upside down, establish the Kingdom of God, and proclaim its presence within, around, and among (Matthew 25:32-46, Mark 16:15-20, Luke 17:20-21, Acts 17:6, Acts 20:24, Romans 1:8-12,17, Romans 3:22, 1 Corinthians 9:19-23, 2 Corinthians 4:1-7, 2 Corinthians 3:3, Ephesians 4:5, Hebrews 12:10-14, 1 Peter 4:12-19).

- **We believe there is one baptism, unto repentance, in water:** it unites us to Christ, in His death, and is symbolic of raising us to new life in Him (Mark 1:4, Matthew 28:19-20, John 3:3-7, Acts 2:1-38, Acts 8:12-40, Acts 9:18, Acts 18:8, Acts 19:4-5, Romans 6:4,

Ephesians 4:5, Colossians 2:11-12, 1 Peter 3:21-22).

- **We believe there is one body:** this bond we share as believers is an apostolic fellowship, one held by the early church, and living, real, and visible today. It is one that is called to walk humbly, gently, patiently, and bearing with one another in love (Matthew 16:18, Matthew 18:15-20, Matthew 26:26-30, Mark 14:22-26, Luke 22:12-20, John 17:1-26, Acts 2:41-47, Acts 9:31, Acts 12:5, Acts 15;4, Acts 16:5, 1 Corinthians 1:2,10, 1 Corinthians 10:1-33, 1 Corinthians 11:18-34, 1 Corinthians 12:14-20,27-28, 1 Corinthians 16:19, Ephesians 2:14-16, Ephesians 3:10-11,21, Ephesians 4:2,4,25, Ephesians 5:27-32, Colossians 3:15, Hebrews 10:23-25, Hebrews 12:24).

- **We believe in living a life worthy of the calling we have received:** we are citizens of heaven and the Kingdom of God, which is the Kingdom of heaven manifest on earth. It is this that we promote, proclaim, and believe shall lead to life (2 Samuel 7:16, Psalm 22:28, Psalm 45:6, Psalm 103:19, Psalm 145:12-13, Matthew 3:2, Matthew 5:3-13, Matthew 6:10-13, Matthew 6:33, Matthew 11:12, Matthew 18:4, Mark 1:15, Luke 1:33, Luke 9:2, Luke 9:60, Luke 17:20-21, John 18:36, Romans 14:17, 1 Corinthians 4:20, Ephesians 4:1, 2 Peter 1:11, Revelation 1:9, Revelation 11:15).

- **We believe in one hope, to which we are called:** Jesus Christ, as faithful to His promises, died, rose, and shall come again. For this, we proclaim His Kingdom (Matthew 24:36-44, Matthew 25:1-13, John 14:1-3, Acts 1:11, Ephesians 4:4, Philippians 2:24, 1 Thessalonians 4:13-18, Titus 2:13, Hebrews 9:28, James 5:7, 2 Peter 3:10, 1 John 2:28, Revelation 22:20).

- **We believe in the Word of God:** both the Scriptures (written word of God) and *logos* (revelation, understanding, precept) that we may understand God's direction and purposes for us. We see experience precedes knowledge, production precedes experience, and existence before essence (Deuteronomy 4:10, Joshua 3:9, 2 Samuel 22:31, Psalm 119:42-44, Ecclesiastes 12:9-10, Isaiah 28:9-13, Matthew 8:8, Matthew 13:19-23, Luke 1:2, Luke 4:21, Luke 11:28, Luke 24:27, John 1:1,14, John 2:2, John 8:51, John 19:28,36, Acts 4:31, Acts 13:49, Romans 4:3, Romans 16:26, 1 Corinthians 12:8, 1 Timothy 4:13, 2 Timothy 2:15, 2 Timothy 3:15-17, James 2:8, Hebrews 4:12-13, 2 Peter 1:20, 1 John 2:5-14).

- **We believe the House of God is for any who seek Him:** we welcome all to come and partake of all God has for us, as His people. We walk in the principle of inclusion; that God calls "whosoever," and "whosoever" comes is welcome. We are more than just an institution or incorporation; we are found family. We stand as a collective of Christian believers who, much like the early church, has become "found family" in a hostile world that doesn't always understand who we are. Our acceptance is here. Our love is here. Our place is here with God and our spiritual family (Isaiah 56:5-7, Jeremiah 31:3, Haggai 2:5-9, Matthew 7:1-20, Luke 6:42, John 6:37, Romans 2:11, Romans 12:13, Romans 14:1-4, Romans 15:7, Hebrews 13:2, 1 Peter 4:9, 1 John 3:15, Revelation 22:16-17).

MISSION STATEMENT

Sanctuary International Fellowship Tabernacle - SIFT seeks to provide a place of spiritual refuge; a place where God can dwell, living and active in the hearts and presence of those who are His people. We believe that as the Kingdom of God is within, among, and around believers (Luke 17:20-21), the Kingdom of God should be made manifest, powerful, living, and active when those who seek Him come together in one place. We believe this happens as we come with open hearts to cry, "Abba, Father!" (Romans 8:15), as we extend our hearts, our hands, and our service to both heaven and our neighbor, in grace, truth, and love.

As a result, we are all about creating connection: Love of God for those who seek it (John 3:16, Galatians 2:20, 1 John 4:9-11); family for those who need it (Psalm 68:6; Ephesians 2:19-22); support for those who desire it (1 Thessalonians 5:11, 1 Peter 4:8-10); and purpose for those who pray to develop it (Exodus 9:16, Romans 8:28, Philippians 2:12-13). It is our desire to remind all people that with God, all things are truly possible to those who believe (Matthew 19:26, Mark 9:23, Mark 10:27, Romans 8:31, Philippians 4:13).

VISION STATEMENT

We seek a new day in the Kingdom of God, one that is relevant for our times and still connects us to the "ancient paths," so we never forget our history, nor where we have come from (Proverbs 23:10, Isaiah 30:21, Jeremiah 18:15, Jeremiah 25:5). We believe the Kingdom of God becomes a reality, one soul, one impacted life, and one loving action at a time. Here in this place of spiritual safety and truth, we ourselves learn how to better exemplify our call as temples of the Holy Spirit (1 Corinthians 3:9, 1 Corinthians 6:19-20), thus making us a chosen generation, a royal priesthood, a holy nation, a peculiar people, and a holy Body of believers, one in faith, hope, and love (Ephesians 4:1-32, 1 Peter 2:9).

SANCTUARY PROGRAMS

Sanctuary offers several programs to help our members find a sense of spiritual purpose as they worship God and connect to one another. Our programs include:

- Weekly worship services, open to all
- Regular Bible Study
- Daily devotional (home) groups
- Sanctuary Spaces (public forum events)
- SIFT Leadership Program
- Metanoia Sunday School
- LOGOS Youth Ministry
- Plaid Place Children's Church
- Young Adult Ministry

INFORMATION TO HELP US SERVE YOU

We are excited to get to know you! To serve you better, we ask you provide us with the following information through our website or app through our Membership Form. We do not sell or share info to anyone, we do not spam or flood inboxes with emails, and we do not harass by phone.

- Name
- Preferred pronouns
- Birthday
- Mailing address
- Email address
- Phone number
- Allergies (such as to food or scents)
- Sensory or physical issues (sensitivity to light or sound, physical pain)

ABOUT THE AUTHOR

Dr. Lee Ann B. Marino, Ph.D., D.Min., D.D. (she/her  or they/them) is "everyone's favorite theologian" leading Gen X, Millennials, and Gen Z with expertise in in leadership training (including Ephesians 4:11 ministry structure and development, protocol and ministry logistics), queer theology (including inclusivity, non-binary, feminist, and female apologetics) typology, pneumatology, conceptual theology, comparative religion, and apostolic theology. She has served in ministry since 1998, was ordained as a pastor in 2002 and as an apostle in 2010. She founded what is now Spitfire Apostolic Ministries in 2004. Under her ministry heading Dr. Marino is founder and overseer of Sanctuary International Fellowship Tabernacle - SIFT (the original home of National Coming Out Sunday) and Chancellor of Apostolic University. A graduate of Apostolic Preachers College (with concentrations in theology, philosophy, religion, and ministry), Dr. Marino has served as a preacher, teacher, prelate, missionary, scholar, songwriter, and worship leader and dancer. In acknowledgement of her extensive work in the apostolic, she has been called "the greatest apostle in the modern church." A needed voice, Dr. Marino's embrace of spiritual issues (both technical and intimate) has found its home among Christians seeking answers today.

Affectionately nicknamed "the Spitfire," Dr. Marino has spent over two decades in "every Pentecostal denomination under the sun." After an early history of abuse and trauma, a college religion project led her to "get saved the first time" in 1999. She was immersed in a spiritual world of spiritual gifts and a powerful call to ministry, sometimes in situations that worked – and in others that went awry. After many years of trying to fit within Charismatic, Holiness, Full Gospel, Oneness, Apostolic, and non-denominational churches, Dr. Marino embraces the identity of neo-Apostolic: a division of modern Pentecostal understanding designed to provide spiritual insight in modern culture.

With a mandate to become "all things to all people," Dr. Marino has preached throughout the United States, Puerto Rico, and Europe. Her experiences have taken her to over five hundred religious services and experiences throughout the years (Christian and non-Christian alike) for experience, knowledge, and ministry. A history maker in her own right, she has spent over two decades in advocacy, education, and work for and within minority spiritual communities (including African American, Hispanic, and LGBTQ+). She served as the first woman on all-male synods, councils, and panels or as the first preacher or speaker welcomed of a different race, sexual orientation, or identity. Today, Dr. Marino's work extends to over one hundred countries as she hosts the popular *Kingdom Now*, *Kingdom Moments*, and *Kingdom Lessons* podcasts and is author of over thirty-five books. She has had four bestselling titles within their subject matter on Amazon: *Understanding Demonology, Spiritual Warfare, Healing, and Deliverance: A Manual for the Christian Minister*; *Ministry School Boot Camp: Training for Helps Ministries, Appointments, and Beyond*; *Surrounded By So Great a Cloud of Witnesses: Women of Faith Who Revolutionized History*; and *Ministering to LGBTQs – and Those Who Love Them*.

Known to those she works with as spiritual mom, teacher, leader, confidant, and friend, Dr. Marino continues to transform, receiving new teaching, revelation, and insight in this thing we call "ministry." Through years of pressing and spiritual growth, Dr. Marino stands as herself, here to present what God has given to her for any who have an ear to hear. As a public icon, Dr. Marino advocates for healthy body image (curvy/full-figured), queer representation (demisexual/aromantic), and albinism awareness, as a model. Her main website is www.kingdompowernow.org.

Made in the USA
Columbia, SC
04 November 2022

70439054R10067